D1070793

GEOFF HAMILTON
THE COMPLETE GARDENER

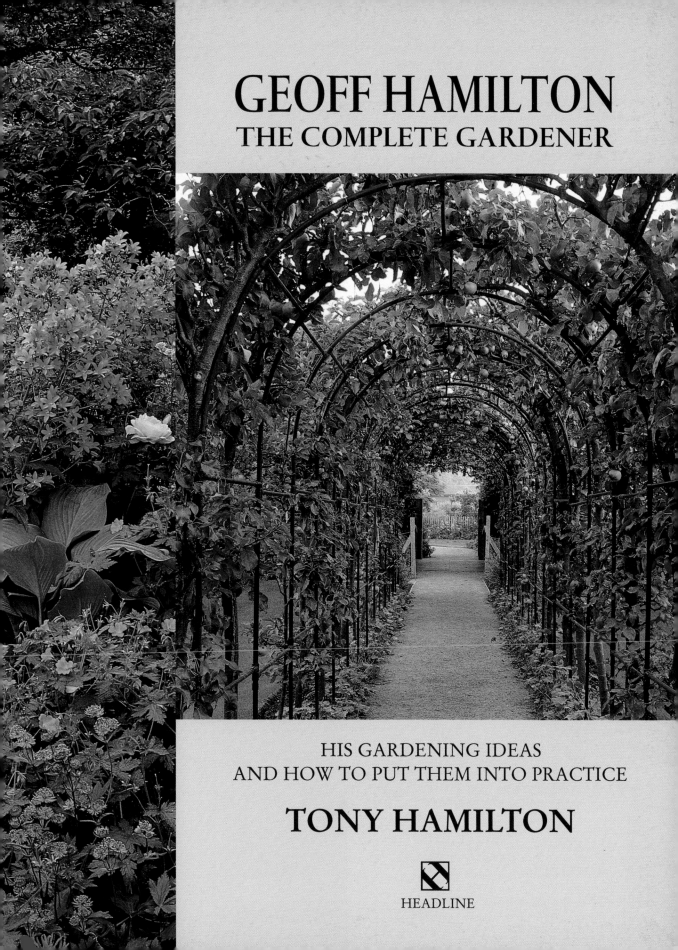

GEOFF HAMILTON
THE COMPLETE GARDENER

HIS GARDENING IDEAS
AND HOW TO PUT THEM INTO PRACTICE

TONY HAMILTON

HEADLINE

First published in 2000
by HEADLINE BOOK PUBLISHING

Tony Hamilton would be happy to hear from readers
with their comments on the book at the following e-
mail address: tony@pta-ltd.com

10 9 8 7 6 5 4 3 2 1

British Library Cataloguing in Publication Data
Hamilton, Tony
Geoff Hamilton: the complete gardener
1. Gardening
I. Title
635

ISBN 0747271402

All photographs are by Stephen Hamilton, except
Richard Adams p.201; David Austin Roses p.198
(below); David Bevan pp.31, 38, 49 (centre);
FLPA/Martin Withers p.62 (below); Garden Picture
Library/M. Watson pp.64,65; HDRA/D.Lawson
p.199; Holt Studios/N. Cattlin p.53; Plantlife pp.62
(top), Plantlife/Jane Smart 200; Jason Smalley p.58;
Woodfall Wild Images pp.29, 60, 61.

Edited by Anne Askwith
Designed by Prue Bucknall
Picture research by Mel Watson
Garden plans by Adam Frost
Illustrations by Michael Hill

Printed and bound in Italy by G. Canale & C. S.p.A.

HEADLINE BOOK PUBLISHING
A division of Hodder Headline
338 Euston Road
London NW1 3BH
www.madaboutbooks.co.uk
www.hodderheadline.com

endpapers: Seaton Meadows painted by Carol Hamilton
page 1: Geoff relaxes in one of his many flower-covered
arbours.
page 2: One of the magnificent borders surrounding
'Versailles', Geoff's earliest development at Barnsdale.
page 3: The fruit walk, once the exit and today the entrance
to Barnsdale Gardens.
page 4: Geoff working in his beloved Barnsdale garden, from
which he derived his deepest satisfaction and joy.

CONTENTS

Introduction

My brother Geoff was a romantic. He would claim that with his job, his family, his house and his garden, he lived in a state of ecstasy. A little overblown you may think, but that was how Geoff really felt. And, as if to make matters more complex and disturbing for the many people who loved him, he was also incurably sentimental. He once confessed to me that he occasionally got a lump in his throat when listening to *The Archers*. Well, I don't think they come more sentimental than that! This combination of romance and sentimentality gave him an enormous generosity of spirit. He and I would often sit together and puzzle over why we had been given so much whilst others had so little, and that sense of the unfairness of life was why he had an urge to share what he had with others – his knowledge, his skills, the products of his garden and even his money when he could. Nobody was insignificant to Geoff. Nobody in need was ever turned away.

He was also a very funny man. His insatiable thirst for fun and laughter and the great joy that seemed to follow in his wake, wherever he went and whoever he was with, are some of the things I miss most about him. He could cut through pomposity and affectation without a hint of cruelty, in a way that left even the subject of his irony laughing.

But he was not just a funny, sentimental romantic; he was also a philosopher who thought carefully and rationally about life and cared deeply about improving its quality. He loved nature and he loved plants. We were brought up in the country and would spend all our time either in our garden at home or wandering the woods and the fields, often sleeping rough in home-made shelters, eating what we had caught or picked from the abundance of free food that surrounds us. By the time we were fourteen we knew the names of every wild plant in the book, where to look for them and what use to make of them, if in need. But Geoff had something of the Red Indian in him, I think, because he would often admonish me for picking plants I didn't need to eat or cutting trees I didn't need for shelter and, in later life, for shooting small birds – a practice I quickly stopped when he drew my attention to what I was doing. He would argue that plants and animals should be treated with as much respect as people. He grew up to be occasionally angry about the way we are led, by politicians and businessmen, to spoil the great beauty that surrounds us in pursuit of a fast buck, and so he became passionate about sharing with others the joy he found in the countryside and in his garden.

All these qualities made him an outstanding gardener and gave him the

Opposite: Tony gathers Swiss chard from a bounteous crop in his own garden.

Four generations of the family – Great Grandma, Grandma, Mother and the three boys, Mark (standing), Geoff (kneeling right) and Tony (kneeling left).

confidence and the ability to communicate his ideas to others. Through writing articles for newspapers and magazines, books and broadcasting, mainly on the BBC television programme *Gardeners' World* and in individual series such as *Geoff Hamilton's Cottage Gardens*, he did this phenomenally successfully, as his outstandingly large and loyal following shows.

This book is about his philosophies and how he built them into his beloved garden at Barnsdale, the place where most of his *Gardeners' World* programmes were made and his home for sixteen years, which he shared with Lynda, his wife. He also shared his ups and his downs with Lynda, trying out his ideas on her, venting his spleen at idiotic politicians with her, railing at greedy industrialists with her, tearing around the country on plant-finding missions with her, singing with her, laughing with her and generally sharing his ecstasy with her, his soul mate and weeder-in-chief.

It is about the constant discussions he and I would have about the subjects that were dear to our hearts. It is about the battles he fought to try to bring some sense of order and peace into our daily lives by rejecting the continuous and frantic chase after profit to nurture and preserve some of the values that have been given to us by nature. It is about his urgent desire to serve the so-called 'working man', to help ordinary men and women enjoy the pleasures that he knew were available to them. He had learned from when he was a boy the unparalleled joy and satisfaction to be gained from bending your back in 'honest toil', from getting your hands deep into some good soil and from building a creation of your own, however modest it may be. He also knew the therapeutic effect of coming home from a harassing or tedious day's work and getting out amongst the good, kindly friends which grow in your garden and join together to smooth your troubles away.

And it is about gardening. I have tried to explain some of Geoff's experiences and ideas. I have tried to trace the way in which Geoff pursued each of his passions, what inspired him to build his best gardens, and how he conceived, planned and constructed them. I have tried to explain some of the practical ways in which he turned his dreams into reality and some of his inventive notions for making life in the garden easier, more appealing and more productive.

This has been an exacting task. Geoff and I were identical twins who lived together or near each other for fifty-odd years, until he died in

August 1996, and we were very close and discussed his work a great deal, so I got pretty good at thinking what he was thinking. But it has not always been possible to be entirely accurate about exactly what went on in his head. So, gentle reader, please accept some poetic licence about the detail of his thoughts. I have been liberal with my interpretation on a few occasions but I know the meat of it is correct.

I hope that in this book I have succeeded in putting across the essence of Geoff Hamilton – his ideals, his work and the man himself. And I hope, too, that you will get from it some ideas for your own garden. For that reason, as well as passing on many of Geoff's tips I have included some basic gardening information to help you to translate those ideas into reality. Geoff was a complete gardener, from the top of his head to the soles of his muddy old boots, and it was undoubtedly the joy and contentment he found at Barnsdale that made him complete. If this book can generate among its readers that joy and contentment, that would be the greatest and most appropriate tribute I could ever make to a man who is greatly missed.

Geoff's greatest delight was to sit in one of his arbours, surrounded by flowers, humming insects and singing birds, relaxing between spells of hard work.

In the beginning

HOW BARNSDALE WAS BORN

Barnsdale was not always where it is now. Geoff's part in *Gardeners' World* began in a much smaller garden about half a mile away from the present Barnsdale. The little house he lived in is still there, but the land now belongs to a country club and there is little trace of the work that he did to make it into an oasis of great beauty. A pity, but country clubs will be country clubs. That garden was also called Barnsdale and Geoff took the name with him when he moved, to avoid confusing his viewers.

In late 1983, when he heard that the house that is now called Barnsdale was coming on to the market, Geoff, in great excitement, and in the dark, went immediately to see it. Like a practised burglar, with a shaded torch in his hand, he crept around the outside of the large, stone Victorian farmhouse and peered through one of the windows. He was amazed to see a group of hippie-like people sitting around a large log fire, no furniture, and violent purple and green psychedelic painting on the wall. He and I got to know these people eventually and we became great friends. We discovered that they grew neither flowers nor vegetables, but I still suspect that they grew something they found more exciting.

But that night he simply slunk back to his cottage with his adrenaline pumping as he thought through the possibilities. He slept little and planned to go to see the house the following morning. What he found in the daylight was exactly what he had hoped for – a sturdy, four-square stone-built Victorian farmhouse with big sash windows, some of them still shuttered with the original pine shutters. When he was invited in, a quick look round assured him that he had found his Shangri-la. He walked up a wide hall, paved with old York stone, into a big, old-fashioned kitchen that was later to serve as the favourite meeting place for all the BBC and Catalyst Television crews. A large, high-ceilinged sitting room led off the kitchen and a similar splendid dining room was adjacent. Of course they all needed lots of attention, but Geoff was never daunted by such a trifle. Through the kitchen window he glimpsed a paved, walled courtyard, beyond which was a small, overgrown kitchen garden.

But best of all was outside the house. He was led past a huge stone-built barn, with great wagon doors and a set of loose boxes built at right angles. Just beyond were five acres of flat land covered in nettles, ragwort and coarse grasses. The whole property was bordered from the quiet road by an avenue of majestic trees of all types, alive with the sound of birds and other wildlife. It was Geoff's idea of paradise – quiet, still and no neighbours. There was a lot of work to do inside the house, let alone getting the land into some kind of shape for a television programme – and he could hardly wait to start.

The house and land were priced at £100,000 and Geoff had £8 in the bank. In the absence of our father, who had died shortly before, I took on his role and wagged a fatherly finger at him, advising him not to be tempted to make an offer. Oh how glad I am that he ignored my advice! Nothing ever seemed to daunt Geoff. He toddled quietly to the bank and, with his customary audacity and the help of a slightly exaggerated letter from his BBC producer, somehow he managed to persuade the bank to lend him the money. A few weeks later, after all the legal arrangements and much impatience on Geoff's part, he was handed the key and became the proud owner of Barnsdale, his heart's desire. Immediately, bubbling with enthusiasm, he rang me to tell me of his success and invited me up to see it.

So next day I drove up to his new empire, with a sinking feeling about the size of the task he had taken on and the financial risk he was taking. When I arrived, and saw how much renovation both the house and the land needed, I felt my misgivings had been fully justified.

'What's the soil like, Geoff?' I asked.

'Oh fine,' he said. 'Look, I've got a sample.' He showed me a sample he had taken with a soil auger. It was thick, shiny, slippery clay that I thought would be better for pottery than for gardening.

Geoff and I had always looked out for each other and I began to feel anxiety rising like an alien creature in my stomach. I could not help thinking of the place he had left – established, full of sumptuous planting and inventive landscaping, and, best of all, cheap.

'Geoff,' I said, 'I just don't see where you're going to start. And how you propose to sustain a television programme with your land in this condition, I just can't imagine.'

I was forgetting Geoff's stubbornness and determination. He just smiled at me – a frustrating, audacious little grin. 'Don't worry, boy. I'll be all right.'

This was typical Geoff. The fact is that he wasn't always all right. He'd had a few disasters in his early career, but he had the happy knack of being able to shrug them off, make a few bad jokes about his own inadequacy and simply get on with the next project. Even so my concerns mounted and I determined to keep a pretty close eye on him. But Geoff was blissfully untroubled by any possibility of failure and simply rolled up his sleeves and got started.

MAKING ORDER FROM CHAOS

Geoff's first job was to get a local agricultural contractor to mole plough the land. A mole plough is a bullet-shaped device, mounted on a heavy stem, which can be pulled through land at a depth of about 45cm (18in), to break up the upper layers, which in this case were heavily compacted, and to leave a drainage channel beneath.

Next he got the contractor to plough the land, turning over the soil and burying the weeds. This left it looking as little like a garden as you could possibly imagine. It could have been worked down enough to grow a fair crop of wheat or barley, but Geoff's vision of a fine floral future looked a long way off.

While this work was going on, each evening, for about a week, Geoff would walk, alone, around his land, just thinking about what he was going to do with it. He told me that he wanted to build one of the classic gardens of England — a place to which people would want to come from far and wide. I still wonder if, even then, he had seen the future that he really wanted for Barnsdale — a place that people could come to for inspiration and advice so that they could find the kind of contentment through gardening that he had found.

After the field at Barnsdale had first been ploughed, Geoff faced a daunting task.

13

After each of his perambulations he would return to the house and, on the kitchen table, draw designs and layouts for the centrepiece of the garden. He knew he would have to build the garden gradually that at this stage it couldn't all be planned, because the *Gardeners' World* programmes were to be filmed there and he would have to respond to the demands of each new television programme, but he wanted to start with a design for a large area close to the house. At the end of the evening the kitchen floor would be strewn with screwed-up paper and he would retire with no final plan but with emerging ideas.

After a week of drawing and discarding and drawing again, he had decided. This first development was to be not only the centrepiece of his garden but a celebration of his new stewardship of the land and the fact that this was a place where he could build his career in television and journalism. So he decided against the intimate style of garden that he was later to build over the rest of his land. The centrepiece had to be a grand gesture. He had seen the sensational formal gardens at Versailles and these gave him his inspiration: he would build a mini-Versailles. This part of the garden is still referred to by the staff as 'Versailles'.

The house was surrounded by a small walled garden, beyond which lay the land that was to be the new garden. He decided to knock a hole in the wall and install a well-made, wrought-iron gate, so that it could be seen through, and then create a long straight vista with grass, edged on each side by large herbaceous borders, to carry the eye down to a feature at the end. Hedges would be planted around the feature to ensure that the eye was not distracted by views of the other gardens which he knew would be required for his television work. He decided that an element of surprise should be maintained: Geoff was a great man for surprises, believing that every corner you turned in the garden had to offer a different experience and a delight. So he would build connecting paths from one garden to another but, at the same time, he would keep the gardens hidden from each other, so as to develop an air of intimacy and uniqueness about them.

In the early days at Barnsdale Geoff spent a great deal of his time at the business end of his rotavator.

WORKING THE SOIL

Geoff's next task was to run his big rotavator over the ploughed land to break it down. He already had his own machine, but if you wish to do this kind of large-scale work yourself and haven't got a rotavator, you can hire one from any good tool hire company. If you're working on virgin or compacted land, make sure the machine is at least five horsepower and has a soil hood at the back. You will also need a pick-up truck to get it home and some strong boards, supported underneath, to get the machine on and off the truck. Alternatively, you can get in a reliable contractor to do it for you, which is much easier and not expensive. Do make sure the contractor has a sizeable machine.

Having got himself a clear, workable area, Geoff marked out the lawn and the surrounding beds.

LAYING THE LAWNS

As he'd already rotavated the whole area, the next stage in preparing the ground for the lawn was just a matter of raking the soil down roughly and then consolidating, as grass seed likes a firm base in which to anchor its roots. If your soil lacks organic matter, as Barnsdale's did, rake in a 5cm (2in) layer of coir or garden compost and if it is heavy do the same with a layer of coarse grit. Consolidation is best done by the power of the foot. No rollers or boards – they just do not have the same effect. You need to tread over the whole area, with your weight on your heels, so that the soil beneath becomes really firm. It is one of the funniest and most inelegant sights to watch somebody doing this – aggrieved husbands or wives might find this a rewarding job to delegate to their partner, for the purposes of one-upmanship. I have to admit that I took the opportunity to visit Geoff at Barnsdale to witness him doing this, waddling duck-like over the ground. We used to enjoy laughing with each other a lot but there is an added piquancy to laughing at each other.

When this rather tedious and tiring job was done, it was time to rake the area down again, to get the levels right, incorporating about two handfuls of fertilizer to every square metre/square yard. Geoff taught me a useful lesson about raking down. To do this job most people hold the rake a long way from their body and make balletic lunges at the soil; but if you keep the rake almost vertical and close to your feet you will be surprised at how much more control you have, and how much more quickly the job can be done. Don't forget that the soil level needs to be at least 2.5cm (1in) above the level of any surrounding paving, for ease of mowing.

Then sow the seed – such as a good ryegrass seed – at the rate of about 25–35g/1–1½oz per square metre/yard. You may need to mark out the measurements of the first row to give you a guideline but you will soon get familiar with the quantity required, and quantity is not all that critical anyway. Finally the seed should be raked in with a spring-tine rake to cover

Raking the soil.

Consolidation by foot.

Sowing grass seed.

Removing surplus turf
with a knife, to ensure
a good fit.

it with soil. You should then put a sprinkler on the lawn. You should ensure that the soil never dries out completely until you give the lawn its first cut, when it is about 7cm/3in high. Raise the mower blades to their highest point and progressively lower them until they are about 2.5cm (1in) above soil level.

If you lay a turf lawn, the consolidation and raking-down process is exactly the same, but in this case you should always work from boards – never walking on prepared soil or laid turf. Lay the longest row, tapping it flat with the back of a rake, and then lay strips all around the perimeter of the lawn. Next place the board on the first row and lay the next row against it, tapping down as you go. When you get to the end of the row, lay the last turf against the one you laid on the perimeter and cut off the surplus with a knife. When this has been completed you can stand back and admire an instant lawn.

The greatest mistake new gardeners make with new turf is to let it dry out, in which case it will shrink and curl and you will be very disappointed. It is vital to keep the turf wet, so don't do it just before you go on holiday or when a hosepipe ban is in operation, or you may experience a disaster. Apply a sprinkler liberally, for about two hours in the same place, so that it gets a really good soaking. Watering with a watering can is simply not enough, unless you have a very small patch of turf.

PREPARING THE BORDERS

While it is not necessary to cultivate deeply for sowing grass, it is a different matter for preparing ornamental borders – particularly if the soil is as heavy and unfriendly as it was at Barnsdale.

So it was sleeves rolled up, spit on the hands and down to the double digging (see page 140). Geoff's view was that this preparation of the soil is the most important stage in gardening. And he was always mindful of the fact that in any new bed you only get this opportunity once, because after this stage you are going to plant with permanent planting, which you cannot remove.

PLANTING TREES

It was very important for Geoff to move the work on the garden along quickly, because he had to have something interesting to show his viewers on *Gardeners' World* by the spring, so he had to have a garden that looked fairly well established by then. So as soon as he had prepared the soil he began planting. His first job was to give the garden some height by planting trees.

Trees not only provide delicate shade to shelter plants (and those who plant them) from the sun, but they carry the eye up and down, removing that dull, flat aspect that one sometimes sees in gardens, especially small ones. So, trees should be the starting point when planting a new garden and in an established garden, however tiny your plot may be, it is worth trying to find room for a tree – or maybe a few. If you plant them at the right distance apart you may live to be very grateful as you swing lazily in your hammock in your senior years. The most common mistake the tree planter makes, and I know because I've done it so many times myself, is to plant trees too close together. It's always advisable to look up the height and width of a tree before buying it and taking the mature width into account when you plant. At first the tree will look small and insignificant, but as the years pass you will be pleased with your foresight.

It is probably best to buy bare-rooted trees from a nursery, for planting between early winter and early spring, but container-grown trees are readily available and, though more expensive, will do as well and can be planted at any time. If you buy them bare-rooted you will generally get a stronger, more developed tree. Remember to keep the roots protected from the wind and sun, while the tree is out of the ground awaiting planting, so that the tiny root hairs, which give life to the tree, are not damaged.

Remember that a tree will need a big planting hole – much bigger than the root ball. Soil preparation is important, although it will not normally be necessary to condition the soil you dig out of the hole, unless it is very heavy and sticky. The main thing is to dig the hole big enough to provide a good run for the roots and deep enough so that you can plant the tree at the depth it was growing at the nursery. If you do not dig the hole wide enough it will become a sump for all the drainage water and the tree will not thrive.

If you are planting a container-grown tree it will not be possible to get the tree close enough to an upright support, because of the size of the root ball. So, in this case plant the tree first and drive in a short stake at forty-five degrees, so that it can support the bottom third of the stem of the tree. Remember that the purpose of the stake is not only to keep the tree upright but to prevent movement at the bottom of the stem.

Geoff chose to plant some fairly common but interesting

Tying a bare-rooted
tree to an upright stake
with a plastic tree tie.

PLANTING A BAREROOTED TREE

Drive a stake into the middle of the hole before you plant, so that it will come about one third of the way up the trunk. This will keep the base of the tree solid whilst allowing just enough swaying to strengthen both the stem and the root system.

Plant the tree and fill the hole with a little compost. Shake the trunk up and down to settle the compost.

Fill the hole with soil, firming it in with your boot. Finally tie the tree to the stake with a tree tie.

trees, which would be easily obtainable by the majority of his viewers and readers, and would provide fascinating changes through the year. These included a silver birch, *Betula utilis*, which has pure white bark that peels as it ages; the crab apple, *Malus tschonoskii*, whose glossy leaves turn brilliant shades of red, orange and purple in autumn; and the common hornbeam, *Carpinus betulus*, which has a fluted trunk, pale green catkins in spring and leaves which turn yellow and green in autumn, when it produces winged nuts – food for squirrels.

He also planted some more unusual trees to give added interest to the garden. Sometimes known as Harry Lauder's walking stick, *Corylus avellana* 'Contorta' has branches twisted and contorted into fantastic shapes (hence the name). *Cotoneaster* 'Cornubia' was planted mainly because it is evergreen, except in the most exposed conditions, and therefore provides some interest in the winter; it also has a mass of white flowers in spring, which are followed by copious bunches of red berries in autumn. The tulip tree, *Liriodendron tulipifera*, is a big tree, which has unusually shaped, lobed leaves and flowers of a delicate greenish-white shade in summer. It does take many years to flower, but Geoff had decided that this was his promised land, and he could wait.

HEDGING

Geoff thought long and hard about the hedging he would use to surround

Versailles. It is sensible to consider carefully a feature that you are going to have to live with for a long, long time and there is a wide variety of hedging plants to choose from. He wanted something to provide a dense backdrop to contrast with his borders, whilst at the same time being interesting in its own right. He ruled out the dreaded Leyland cypress (x *Cupressocyparis leylandii*) as being too hungry, too big, too uninteresting and altogether unacceptable. He did consider yew (*Taxus baccata*), but he wanted something that would establish a little faster. Privet (*Ligustrum ovalifolium*) was out because it is uninteresting and, being very hungry, would, he felt, impoverish his soil. In the end he chose beech (*Fagus sylvatica*) because it establishes fairly fast, gives a wonderfully dense growth in summer, and turns russet and yellow in autumn. It is also very amenable to trimming, thickening in the centre to give a very dense hedge with a distinctly architectural shape, if well cut. The hedges are now a fine example of what can be done with expert care.

Hedging plants are much cheaper if they are obtained bare-rooted, in which case they will need to be planted between November and March. They can be bought in containers, but at much greater cost, and can be planted at any time. Either way, the successful gardener's most honoured companion, patience, is required to see them mature into a useful hedge that is worth looking at.

The first job in planting a hedge is to ensure that the soil is well prepared, to give your plants a good start. Remember, you don't get two chances to do this. Dig a trench at least 1m (3^1/$_2$ft) wide and, if you have the energy, two spits deep, and use plenty of farmyard manure or compost. Resist the temptation to plant closer than the recommended planting distances; that will only put up the cost of what, in the end, will be an inferior hedge. Some hedging plants, such as privet, sloe, hazel and hawthorn, should be cut back to about 15cm (6in) from the ground immediately after planting, as this will encourage bushier growth and therefore a thicker hedge.

You should feed a hedge in spring with fish, blood and bone fertilizer or chicken manure pellets and then mulch to retain moisture. Then you have the uniquely satisfying job of trimming them. Beech, laurel, hornbeam or conifers should not be trimmed until they have reached the required height, when cutting out the top shoots will limit further growth; then an annual trim is usually sufficient to keep them in order. Other fast-growing hedges such as privet, however, will need regular trips to the barber if they are not to get out of control. Slower-growing hedges such as yew and beech and box will only need trimming once or twice a year. Laurel hedges are best cut with secateurs, a tedious job, but one that avoids the unsightly

Though it may seem an arduous task, nothing repays the effort more than a neatly clipped hedge.

finish caused by cutting the leaves with shears. Fortunately they only need cutting once or twice a year.

Two final points about hedges. First, remember that they can collect a lot of rubbish in the bottom, which will harbour pests and diseases. So give them a good rake out in the autumn, to keep them healthy. Second, I make a plea for you to be kind to your neighbours – however peculiar or irritating you may find them. Everybody has a God-given right to sun and light in their garden, so try not to let your hedge deprive your neighbours of theirs.

GOINGS ON IN THE SHRUBBERY

Once the trees and hedges were in place Geoff's next job was to plant shrubs. Some of these came from his previous garden just up the road and some came from specialist nurseries. Geoff would tour these nurseries in his Land Rover and trailer, and return with both stacked to the gunwales with shrubs of every description. Geoff was a plant junkie all his life. Even as a young man he would often go to see Cornelius (Cor) van Hage, who had a small garden centre at the top of our road, and beg, 'borrow' or sometimes even pay for a plant that he had set his heart on, and he always had 'just the right place to put it'. Cor, who now owns a huge garden centre in Amwell in Hertfordshire, was, for a successful businessman, amazingly soft-hearted and generous to Geoff and always gave in to his entreaties. Perhaps he saw in him a budding replica of himself.

Geoff's shrub planting plan was designed to give basic structure to the garden, with some shrubs introduced for their foliage, others for their colour and some for their shape. He followed the same philosophy that he had with the trees. He planted some common species that his viewers could buy at any garden centre, such as the Japanese snowball bush, *Viburnum plicatum* 'Mariesii', which is clothed in large clusters of white flowers in spring and dark glossy leaves which turn red in autumn; the smoke bush, *Cotinus coggygria* 'Royal Purple', which sets the border on fire with its bright purple leaves and deep pink plumes; *Weigela florida* 'Variegata', a tall, arching shrub bearing deep pink flowers which are a delicate pink-white inside; and *Berberis candidula*, a compact shrub which instantly draws the eye with its bright golden foliage. And he planted some more unusual shrubs to provide interest and talking points – for instance, *Neillia thibetica*, a lovely arching shrub with a great profusion of deep pink flowers in spring and early summer; a tree peony, *Paeonia suffruticosa*, which has large, cup-shaped flowers of a delicate pink-white shade and a deep chocolate spot at the base; and, a plant to provide dramatic architectural structure, *Sarcococca hookeriana*, which is a dense, tall variety of sweet box,

Opposite: This impressive border, packed with trees, shrubs and herbaceous perennials, filters patterns of light through to the long grass 'vista' in Versailles.

Weigela florida 'Variegata'.

Paeonia suffruticosa.

with dark clusters of leaves, tiny white flowers in winter and dark fruits.

He deliberately overplanted, putting shrubs too close together, in the certain knowledge that in two or three years' time he would have to take some of them out again. This was done to establish the garden quickly, so that it could be used by the BBC, but additionally it fitted Geoff's philosophy that gardens are more interesting as well as more beautiful if plants grow into one another, giving a natural and untended look. Of course the other advantage with close planting is that it cuts down the need for weeding. Weeds grow mainly on open ground, so if you cover it up with plants and give them little light they will go next door.

FILLING IN

When all the shrubs were planted, Geoff added a wide variety of herbaceous perennials. Amongst his particular favourites were *Papaver orientale* 'Pizzicato', an amazing semi-dwarf poppy with huge flowers in a wide range from white to scarlet, with characteristic black blotches, and the extraordinary *Rudbeckia occidentalis* 'Green Wizard', which grows to 1.25–1.5m (4–5ft) and has bright green sepals where other plants have petals. Geoff also valued *Acanthus spinosus*, a spectacular plant for late summer colour, having deeply cut, spiny leaves and 45cm (18in) spikes of white and purple flowers, and the red ink plant, *Phytolacca americana*, which presents three great assets in one – ovate mid-green leaves, tinged with purple in autumn, long spikes of white flowers in summer, followed by large black (but poisonous) berries in autumn. He supplemented these with *Sedum spectabile*, which forms a dense clump of fleshy leaves followed by rich pink flowers in autumn, *Euphorbia polychroma* (formerly *E. epithymoides*), a compact shrubby plant with wide yellow bracts in spring, and *Aster novi-belgii* 'Fellowship', a vigorous aster giving a welcome display of pure pink flowers in autumn.

For ground cover he used gently contrasting plants including *Epimedium* x *youngianam* 'Niveum', which has bronze leaves in spring, gradually turning green, and a delicate display of cup-shaped white flowers in spring, as well as *Heuchera micrantha* var. *diversifolia* 'Palace Purple', a clump-forming plant with deep purple leaves and sprays of white flowers.

Even though he overplanted these quite liberally too, there were still sizeable gaps the following spring, which would not be acceptable for filming. So he sowed small areas with hardy annuals to fill these in and add colour and variety to the border. Planting annuals – which complete their life cycle within one growing season – is always a good idea for anybody planting up a new garden and looking for a quick and cheap way to fill it with colour. For a few bob you will have all the packets of seed you need to have a riot of colour for the summer. Annuals also attract beneficial insects. So, even in the first summer, you will have the pleasure of the soothing sound of the bees as well as a home for all the useful predators, such as ladybird larvae and the hoverfly, which consume prodigious quantities of greenfly and other pests. (Why is it that hoverflies, which eat vast meals at every sitting, never get fat? Have you ever seen a fat hoverfly?)

When you buy the seed you will find you are offered two types: hardy and half-hardy annuals. Hardy annuals will withstand a degree or two of frost but half-hardy will not. Hardy annuals are much easier to grow than half-hardy as they can be sown directly into the soil in spring. Half-hardy annuals have to be started in the greenhouse, or on the windowsill if your domestic arrangements will allow.

When they are big enough to handle, the delicate plants will need to be pricked out into another seed tray, at a wider spacing and grown on until ready for 'hardening off' in a cold frame where they can be protected from frost at night. Alternatively, it is possible (but not so satisfying and more expensive), to buy both hardy and half-hardy annuals as seedlings ready to plant out from good garden centres.

All you need to do to grow annuals is to prepare a seed bed and mark it out in crescents (or whatever shape you prefer), so that you can sow a different variety in each. This method will give you drifts of plants, rather than a mixture. One of the things that Geoff taught me was that it is a mistake to buy seed mixtures. You get a much more dramatic and eye-catching effect with drifts of the same colour and variety than you do with a mass of different colours and shapes, all competing with each other for the attention of the beholder. (The same applies to all but the biggest

PLANTING ANNUALS

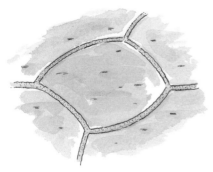 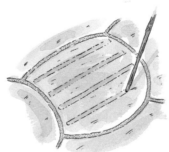 

Sow annuals in spring in 'drifts' of a single colour. Mark out a shape to fit

your design and then draw straight drills across it, 15cm (6in) apart.

Sow the seed thinly and thin out the seedlings to about 15–20cm (6–9in apart).

herbaceous plants. Plant them in clumps of three or four and you'll get a much more pleasing effect.)

The seed is best sown in the spring, in straight drills within the crescent you have marked. This will help you to differentiate the plants from the weeds, which will, of course, both emerge at the same time.

It is best not to use any fertilizer for annuals as this will promote leaf growth at the expense of flowers. A little garden compost or well-rotted manure should be more than adequate. If, like me, you have cats, dogs and rabbits to contend with, just cover them with a piece of wire netting until they are established (the seedlings, I mean, not the cats, dogs or rabbits) and don't forget to keep them well watered during dry weather.

Of course biennials – plants which are sown one year and flower the next, after which they die – are a useful filler, too. Many flower over a long period and some, like sweet williams, have a powerful scent, which will fill your garden. Biennial seeds should be sown in open ground in early summer. When they are big enough to handle, plant them out in rows about 10cm (4in) apart and move them into their final growing positions in early autumn. I have found that if the weather is bad or you have too little space in the autumn, they can be transplanted right up to March without much harm, but the rule should be the earlier the better.

THE FEATURE

When the grass had grown and the planting was beginning to burgeon and show its future promise, it was time for Geoff to consider the feature at the end of the long, straight lawn. He thought about a statue, but felt it might look a bit out of place. He finally settled on an urn, which he could plant to give a blaze of colour against the dark green of the beech hedge.

We made some rather predictable jokes about a 'little Ern with short, fat, hairy legs' but he decided the urn had to make a big, bold statement. So in typical Geoff fashion he dug deep into money he didn't have and bought a fine stone urn from Haddonstone. At about the same time he had begun to be asked to press conferences and meetings, and he felt that, rather than constantly asking to borrow one of my suits, he ought to get one of his own. Well, it was a toss-up between the suit or the urn, because the bank would not stand for both. I feel I need hardly tell you that my suits continued to go out on loan to Geoff for a considerable period – and what annoyed me was that I could not afford to buy an urn!

With great difficulty and considerable back strain we carried the urn down to the bottom of the lawn and proudly lifted it on to its plinth. It was perfect. Geoff planted it up with stately fuchsias and pelargoniums for height and surrounded them with petunias, tumbling nasturtiums, white and blue lobelia and stately grey helichrysum. He was like a boy with a new toy. He would stop in the middle of his lunch to go out for what he called 'admiring time' and come back with a big, Cheshire-cat smile on his face.

It was about this time that Ian Spence took up his post as Geoff's senior gardener and friend. A quiet, unassuming Scotsman, he is equipped with a gardening knowledge second to none and with an ability to work not only hard and steadily but also to the highest standards of quality. Ian leaves a trademark that is unmistakable. If it's really good, it's Ian. Geoff relied on him to work on his own initiative and to take care of all the day-to-day work of a large, extremely busy garden.

The sweeping curve of the pergola, clothed in laburnum, clematis and other climbers, connects Versailles with a perfumed walk to the other parts of the garden.

He has now set up a garden maintenance business which has a full order book and good potential to expand. But, perhaps because of Geoff's influence, Ian discovered another skill. He began to write, initially small articles for local papers and eventually for the *Daily Telegraph*. He also has book projects on the stocks and does some broadcasting. Perhaps he learned more from Geoff than we ever knew.

MAKING THE CONNECTION

Lastly Geoff decided to connect Versailles to the rest of the garden through a pergola as described on page 125, over which he would grow a variety of climbers, some of which would suspend their flowers just above the heads of passers-by, and delight them with the warmth of their colour and perfume. Having prepared the soil well, he used a combination of laburnum, wisteria and honeysuckle, as well as climbing roses planted with clematis, and established a grass walkway under the pergola.

Now the first steps at Barnsdale and the centrepiece of the garden were complete, but beyond it lay five acres of land that had been no more than ploughed. This was Geoff's next challenge for development, and was to be the scene of his passion and mission, organic gardening.

In gloria organicorum

EARLY DAYS

Organic gardening had not always been Geoff's passion – not by any means. When he and I started gardening, which was when we were knee high to a geranium, we would mix our own fertilizer, standing side by side at the bench, in our short trousers, in the old green potting shed at the bottom of the family garden. To do this we would buy 'straights' – basic chemicals – from the chemist or the ironmonger. A dollop of sulphate of potash here, a handful of superphosphate there, all mixed in with a generous dose of sulphate of ammonia, and there we had it. A probably lethal mix, but we did not know that at the time, and it made our plants grow like crazy.

We got the recipes for our fertilizer from books we bought with our precious pocket money from Loveday's, the junk shop in the local town – books by Dr Shewell-Cooper, Arthur Simons, Richard Sudell and the like. We had one favourite, issued by the Royal Horticultural Society, called *The Vegetable Garden Displayed*, and displayed it certainly was. It was full of slightly out-of-focus, black-and-white pictures of earnest men in braces, shirts with no collars and big boots, with purposeful looks on their faces, doing heroic things for the war effort with swedes and cabbages. We devoured it. There was also a strip cartoon in the *Daily Mirror* called 'Mr Digwell', which we would read avidly in every issue. Those were the days when the *Mirror* was a proper socialist paper, so our dear old dad, a rampant socialist, used to take it for the political content – although we often used to catch him having a sly look at Mr Digwell first.

Chemical herbicides and pesticides were not as readily available then as they are today, but whenever we could get them we would spray our plants liberally with noxious substances, many of which have since been banned because they had an unpleasant tendency to kill off the people who used them. In those days there were no labels, no masks, no precautions of any kind. These chemicals didn't only kill people: they also killed ladybirds, hoverflies, hedgehogs, birds, cats and dogs. We used them because we didn't know better. There had been little research into the effects of the use of large quantities of chemicals on the land so we simply didn't understand the consequences.

Geoff's assumption that this practice was the right one was reinforced when he went to college at Writtle, to study horticulture. There he learned long lists of chemical fertilizers, herbicides and pesticides, and the best way

Opposite: This impressive border packed with vegetables and flowering plants is also alive with bees, butterflies and other insects, as well as giving a home to frogs, toads and other small mammals – all nurtured through the protection from harmful chemicals resulting from Geoff's organic policy.

Tony (left) and Geoff (right), at about the age they first became enthusiastic about gardening.

to apply them. He became quite an expert in what chemicals to use in any given circumstance – a budding toxicologist in fact.

Armed with paraquat and dieldrin, he launched himself on to an unsuspecting world, spreading and spraying chemicals at every opportunity and killing off goodness knows what in the process. He continued to do this, with boundless enthusiasm, throughout his early career right up to and including his first years at Barnsdale. In many of his early books he recommends the use of chemicals for all kinds of pests, diseases and weeds, and his television programmes were loaded with advice on spraying, chemical fertilizers, slug pellets and a whole array of grotesque pollutants of one sort or another.

In one of the first BBC books Geoff wrote, *Gardeners' World Vegetable Book*, he says:

In recent years weedkillers have had a bad press. The very word 'herbicide' has become associated with the defoliation of trees in Vietnam, large-scale disasters in Italy and the accidental destruction of crops by spray drift the world over. It's a pity because it really has very little to do with garden weedkillers ... It is true to say that, if they are used to the manufacturer's instructions, they are harmless. And they can be a real boon to both the professional grower and the amateur gardener.

He went on to recommend the use of dalapon for the destruction of couch, a mixture of paraquat and diquat for use on annual weeds and simazine and propochlor as pre-emergence weedkillers. He had in the past also suggested, and used himself, many other substances that are now banned, such as DDT, chlorodene, aldrin and dieldrin.

So how can this be said to equate with his love of nature and his passionate views about the preservation of the environment – let alone his generous-hearted approach to the preservation of people? Well, the plain fact is that he simply didn't know, at the time, what these noxious chemicals could do to wildlife and to the people who used them – and indeed ate them.

THE GREEN CONVERSION
But gradually the light began to dawn. Geoff travelled a lot, read a lot and

met a lot of people during the course of his work and more and more he would run across gardeners with beautiful and productive gardens who refused to use any kind of chemical on their land. And, much to his surprise, he discovered that they were not all the cranks that such people were perceived to be at the time.

One person Geoff particularly admired was Beth Chatto, whose gardens near Colchester, Essex, are a sneak preview of what heaven will be like. Full of colour, structure, shape and foliage, they make you ache to be able to reproduce her effects in your own backyard. No chemical fertilizers of any kind are used. Beth is a compost person. She makes literally tons of it from her 6 hectare (15 acre) garden and buys in load after load of animal manure and straw, all of which is used to mulch her plants and improve the soil. She also covers the soil with a mulch of chipped bark to persuade the weeds that still want to show their faces that they are fighting a losing battle. With all the added nutrients from the organic material she doesn't need to use chemicals to promote strong growth and an abundance of flowers.

A once clear and vibrant stream now frothing and foaming with deadly pollutants.

Geoff also became a good friend of the Henry Doubleday Research Association: the Organic Organisation (HDRA), near Coventry, which is perhaps the major centre for organic research in the UK. Geoff saw that what they were doing there was not only successful but also a great deal cheaper than investing in expensive fertilizers, chemical herbicides and insecticides and the equipment to apply them.

The work being done at the HDRA and his meetings with other organic gardeners and campaigners began to persuade Geoff of the extensive damage that the use of chemicals was doing – to the environment, to wildlife, to the quality of the crops we grow and not least to the people who suffered the consequences.

CHEMICAL FERTILIZERS

It seems such an innocuous action, simply to spread a handful or two of chemicals on the garden and see them disappear. But the consequences are devastating. Chemical fertilizers do untold damage to our environment because they disturb the delicate balance of bacteria in the soil, deplete its structure and leach into waterways, encouraging rampant weed growth and poisoning the water which would otherwise be home to an abundance of wild creatures. Many of our rivers are now just lifeless streams, green with algae and covered in foaming scum, when even a young shaver like me, born before the dramatic rise in the use of chemicals, can remember them as clear, vibrant habitats for an exuberant community of fish, water rats, otters, shellfish, birds and many others and teeming with billions of microscopic creatures on which the fish fed and which kept the water alive.

Poisonous algae have twice, during warm summers, engulfed Rutland Water, a mile from Barnsdale, killing sheep and dogs who drank the water. And this is a reservoir that supplies us with our daily drinking water. That's just one example that happens to be very close to home, but it's happening all over the country as those of us who use chemical fertilizers abandon our stewardship responsibility for our land.

Geoff's views were particularly strong because not only had he seen, and was to show himself, that it is not necessary to use chemical fertilizers – he also realized that it is positively harmful. Chemical growers apply fertilizers to feed the plants, rather than to improve the soil, and instead of improving it; as Geoff observed in his book *Successful Organic Gardening*, 'The practice of replacing organic matter on the land has died out. The result is that the soil is becoming lifeless.' Without organic matter, the soil becomes nothing more than a receptacle for the chemicals and turns into an inert mass, without any of the constituents required for strong, healthy growth. So repeated doses of chemicals are needed, year after year after year, gradually destroying the soil's structure and increasing the pollution of the soil. Using chemical fertilizers instead of improving the soil, whether commercially or in the garden, will have negative effects, even if they make the plants grow bigger. Flower borders will become more difficult to cultivate and less attractive, whilst vegetables have less flavour and fewer health-giving properties. Organic vegetables, on the other hand, are more likely to be sweet and succulent and they'll put hairs on your chest as well.

Far left: Ladybirds and their larvae, wolfing through an infestation of aphids.

Left: Bees are free to gather nectar in a chemical-free garden, pollinating as they go.

Far left: A lacewing, whose larvae feed voraciously on aphids, mites and other small pests. Bizarrely, lacewings sometimes camouflage their bodies with the drained skins of their prey.

Left: Butterflies and moths are not only good pollinators but will also beautify your garden, if not in danger of chemical attack.

CHEMICAL PESTICIDES

Pesticides will kill off almost all the creatures who dine off your plants, but they will also kill off all those who don't. Amongst those will be ladybirds, hoverflies, lacewings, bees, butterflies and a host of others which not only add to the beauty of your garden but will efficiently do the job of pest control, without recourse to the chemical bottle.

Take out the sprayer and with one squirt of chemical spray you can kill millions of your friends. Do it regularly and you will commit genocide on them all – and your garden will begin to decline. Gradually you will lose all your allies and the garden will be occupied by your enemies – so you'll have to step up the assault, which will only make matters worse. This was why Geoff, who had a respect even for the smallest insect, eventually threw his sprayer away to concentrate on

Geoff showed beyond doubt that organic methods can produce luxuriant growth, colour and form, as well as plentiful yields of vegetables without recourse to harmful chemicals.

more friendly ways of dealing with pests and diseases.

Slug pellets kill not only hedgehogs but also thousands and thousands of birds which, if left alone, would provide a Royal Command performance in your garden every day. They can also be passed down the food chain to put paid to your cat if it kills and eats a bird – or any of your pets if the pellets are directly eaten by them.

Chemical methods are used extensively by farmers in the pursuit of more more and more profits, because the supermarkets are pressing them for higher and higher yields, and better colour and uniformity (which are nearly always at the expense of flavour). But the environmental effects are such that, in order to ensure that all your carrots are of uniform size or that there is never a slug mark on your lettuce, they – and we who contribute by buying what they produce – are painstakingly building a ticking time bomb.

ON THE ORGANIC ROAD

Geoff's view was that even if we cannot persuade the farmers to change (although we should continue to try), at least we don't have to add to the problem by bad gardening. Although he felt the organic route was not necessarily the easiest to follow, he was left in little doubt that it was the most beneficial to the environment. He was keen to garden organically himself, and to see if organic gardening methods would keep pests and diseases at bay, and to see if it would improve the beauty of his already beautiful ornamental garden. He also knew that organic gardening would be as close to nature's way as he could get and his empathy with all plants was one of the basic feelings that drove Geoff to do the work he did. He once wrote about his sadness at pulling a weed. 'It's like getting rid of an old friend, and I apologize as I pull it up,' he said.

Although he knew he would meet opposition from his fellow members of the gardening press and those who had an interest in maintaining their commercial position, he also began to feel that perhaps he had a duty to his readers and viewers to let them in on these 'secrets' — for at the time, the mid-1980s, the organic gardeners he had met were the exception rather than the rule and the general public were largely unaware of these arguments. After all, why should they want to spend their hard-earned cash, as well as their time and effort, on smothering their gardens with poisonous chemicals, and in doing so reduce the natural beauty of their gardens and allotments by killing off wildlife and damaging the environment too?

So it was time to put on his armour, mount his trusty steed of a typing chair and unsheath his word processor to go into battle with the press. He also planned an intensive campaign on television, which eventually attracted some trenchant comments from his fellow members of the gardening press and some fairly vitriolic letters from people who clearly had an interest in maintaining their commercial position. But, in the event, it is quite noticeable that, as the organic lobby grows, the response from gardening programmes on both radio and television have begun to soften and the vested interests are beginning to be influenced by the voice of the people they are meant to serve.

ORGANICS ON TRIAL

Whilst Geoff was pretty romantic about his beloved plants, he was hard-headed enough to know that persuading people not to use chemicals would be difficult. For years and years we had been conditioned to believe that as soon as a pest or a fungus appeared it was time to get out the sprayer and squirt a chemical; if a plant looked a little pale and wan the chemical medicine cabinet must hold the answer — a handful of chemicals and it will be home tomorrow. People are still saying it — on television and radio, in gardening books and journals you still find a persistent and pernicious exhortation to reach for the poisons. In the face of such conditioning hard evidence was all the more necessary. He knew that his viewers and readers would soon get impatient with anything that reduced the productivity of their vegetable plots or impaired the look of their ornamental gardens. After all, it is asking a lot of keen gardeners to see their roses covered in greenfly and to stand by and do nothing when, on the shelf in the shed, there is a small bottle that will solve the problem in a trice. He knew that he had to ask for three rare commodities in today's hectic life: patience, determination and time. Even if you wait the five years it takes for the level of natural predators to build up to give adequate control over pests, you still have the problems of pernicious weeds, fungal attack and other diseases, which have no natural predators.

So he knew he had to come up with some answers that would satisfy the doubters and the cynics — and he had to demonstrate that organic gardening was really worth the effort. He had to show that it was possible to have an organic garden that was beautiful and not ravaged by pests and diseases, with the additional rewards of vegetables that no longer tasted like soap powder and a community of wildlife, even in the smallest or noisiest of gardens.

Much against his BBC producer's wishes, he started some trials, growing organically on one plot and chemically on another. And the organic results were a disaster! Caterpillars, slugs, greenfly, carrot fly, blight, black spot — you name it, he had it. But Geoff was a stubborn old beggar and he had been advised by the HDRA that it would take some time for natural predators to build up and for the soil to become vibrant enough to nurture strong, healthy, disease-resistant crops. So the next year, with his producer now puce with rage, he did the trials again. This time the results were still poor — but not quite so poor. So, with his producer now beginning to show some interest, he did it again. After five years his organic crops were flourishing and easily outdoing the crops that had been treated chemically. The chemically treated crops were now looking thin and tired, while his organic crops were not only plump and fit but tasted how vegetables used to taste when Geoff was a boy. I know, because I used to scrounge some from him week by week. It was Geoff's habit to take a walk with Lynda around the garden each evening and, to his immense delight, he noticed that slowly, and almost imperceptibly, the hum of bees was getting louder, the birdsong was increasing, the dog would tentatively unearth the odd hedgehog and the air was full of butterflies, hoverflies and a multitude of other insects.

At last he felt he had cracked organic gardening and, whilst he still had his failures, he decided that in future Barnsdale would be entirely organic. He offered his sprayer to me, but I turned it down because I had been following the master in my own garden and I now felt I had cracked it too.

GETTING DOWN TO EARTH

I think a lot about Geoff when I work in my own garden, and when I am digging or preparing the soil for planting or sowing I hear him saying to me, 'Get your soil right, boy, and the rest will come right.' Wise words. Geoff used to take immense care to see that the soil at Barnsdale was prepared as thoroughly as possible and then kept in fertile condition by good husbandry. We would often smile at the letters he received from his television viewers saying things like, 'It's OK for you – you've got wonderful soil. No wonder you grow such good plants. If you had to work with my heavy clay you couldn't do it.' Obviously they did not know that when Geoff first took over the land at Barnsdale and had it ploughed, the plough turned up glistening furrows of clay so heavy you could hardly lift a spadeful. It was only by shovelling literally tons of farmyard manure, compost and coarse grit in to it that he got it into the fine, friable shape it is now.

A strong believer in knowing where you stand scientifically, Geoff recommended that the first thing to do, particularly if you have a new garden, is to get an analysis of the soil to find out your starting point. This is best done by an independent soil analyst, who will have all the equipment and expertise to do it (you can find the names of soil analysts in the gardening press). You simply need to send the analyst a soil sample, taken from various representative parts of your garden, and you will receive a detailed analysis of soil type and mineral content and some words of advice about how to deal with your plot. You should remember to tell the analyst that you are an organic gardener, so that you are given advice that is relevant to your needs.

After that analysis all that should be necessary is an annual pH test to determine the acidity or alkalinity of your soil. You can do this yourself; testing kits are cheap and can be bought from your local garden centre.

Liberal applications of organic matter can make the most inhospitable soil warm and friendly.

SOIL CONDITIONING

One of the questions Geoff was most frequently asked by viewers and readers was a cry for help about heavy, cold, clay soils. He noticed that these letters often came from people living in new houses. It is quite common for builders to level a large site by bulldozing all the topsoil into one place, and as a result one lucky house buyer gets all the good topsoil while all the rest of the houses on the site are left with the inhospitable subsoil. This is often made worse by the fact that the builders then excavate the foundations for the buildings and spread the spoil, nearly always heavy clay subsoil, over the only patches of topsoil that may be left. They often cover this with a sward of shrinking turf. The buyers think they are getting the makings of a garden, but they have an unpleasant surprise in store.

The viewers' letters complained that they did not seem to be able to lighten such soil without the use of peat, but Geoff avoided this like the plague (see pages 59–71). Being negative was not one of Geoff's weaknesses (perhaps my next book will be about what they were), and his view was that whatever difficulties you may have with your soil they can be rectified by good organic methods. First your soil should be well drained, and this can usually be achieved with plenty of organic matter and a good layer of coarse grit, or you could try growing on raised beds, still incorporating lots of organic matter and grit.

Secondly your plants will need air and nutrients for them to thrive and here again lots of organic matter is the answer. It will not only provide a well-aerated structure but will also encourage earthworms in abundance, who will help to aerate the lower levels; and, with the help of microorganisms which break it down and help to fix nitrogen in the soil, the organic matter will deliver an abundance of plant nutrients, without the risk of pollution.

ORGANIC MATTER

As the use of organic matter was at the heart of Geoff's organic gardening philosophy, I shall list here some of the most common and easily available sources, almost all of which are cheaper than peat.

Garden compost is one of the cheapest and easiest ways to condition soil – and it recycles waste, so it is environmentally friendly as well.

Geoff always recommended making one or two wooden compost bins, using a frame of 5cm x 5cm (2in x 2in) timbers clad with old floorboards, or better still, new timber, if your finances will stand it. There is now some research that suggests that pressure-treated timber, which will last the longest, may allow small quantities of arsenic to leach into your compost. Painting on a preservative is not so durable, but could be safer.

The bin should be about 90cm (36in) square and high. This is big enough for it to build up some heat, which will help the compost to rot down faster. It should have a removable front, so that the compost can be

There are many good, serviceable plastic compost containers on the market, for gardeners who haven't the time or the carpentry skills to make their own.

MAKING A COMPOST BIN

A good-sized compost bin can easily be made from second-hand timber, even if you have only rudimentary carpentry skills. A double bin is useful because it allows you to turn the compost from the first into the second with ease. Some construction suggestions are shown opposite. Remember to paint the bin with a preservative paint to prolong its life.

reached. This is made by nailing two slats of wood to each side, so that the front timbers can slide in between. Finally, you need a hinged lid, covered with a bit of roofing felt, to keep the rain out and the heat in. Some people recommend open sides to let the air in, but Geoff found that these allow the compost to dry out and the results are not as good. Alternatively, and particularly if you have a very small garden, you can buy some very serviceable plastic compost bins from a garden centre.

The compost itself is made from grass cuttings mixed with garden refuse (so long as it is not diseased), weeds (but not pernicious ones) and kitchen waste (uncooked, or it will attract rats). In fact, almost any organic matter can be used as an addition to your compost heap. The other types of organic matter listed below can all be added. Geoff, in one of his books, even recommended old income tax bills as a fruitful source.

Mix it all up well, as the bacteria that break it down like to have some air (who can blame them?) – otherwise you will simply get a slimy mess that will not help the garden. Many gardeners like to use a compost activator, to chivvy the bacteria into action. I don't use one myself, as I find my compost system works well without, but if I were going to I would probably favour pelleted chicken manure (see page 44). It is also good to turn the compost at least twice during its lifetime, by throwing it out of the bin and simply throwing it back in again. This may sound like the kind of work goalers used to give convicts on hard labour, but believe me, it's well worth it.

In this way you should end up after two or three months with a clean, sweet smelling, friable compost. Geoff used to claim that his compost was good enough to eat, although it can now be revealed that I never actually saw him doing so.

There are three other methods of composting, specially designed for the lazy gardener. The first is to make a pile in a corner of the garden and cover it with some old carpet. It is unsightly and slower, but will still result in good compost. The second is to dig a trench in the garden to bury your waste. This will then rot in exactly the same way, and the following year you can grow crops straight on to it, but you need a space that can be left vacant for a year. Or you can spread the raw material for the compost between the rows of vegetables and let it rot down where it is, for digging in in the winter. This is pretty unsightly, but it does have the advantage of mulching the plants and reducing soil compaction as you walk between the rows. I don't do it generally, although I have found it acceptable on a crops like potatoes or broad beans, where the crop itself is soon large enough to cover the offending sight of rotting weeds.

Animal manures The two principle manures Geoff used at Barnsdale were cow and horse manure, both of which are easily obtainable if you live in the country. If you have the space it is best to leave the manure heaped up for a year in a corner of the garden – cover the heap with a sheet of polythene to stop the nutrients leaching out and to let it compost. This is particularly true of horse manure, which tends to be a little too strong for tender roots. Composting will also help to get rid of any toxins that may remain if it contains straw that was sprayed with herbicides or pesticides. Any straw in it needs to be well rotted – and it may be necessary to supplement it with a high nitrogen feed, to help to break it down – because otherwise when used on the soil it will rob it of nitrogen as it continues to rot.

Remember that one of the most popular sports, particularly for youngsters, is horse riding. Look in the *Yellow Pages* and even if you live in a town or city there is sure to be a riding school near you. They may or may not deliver a load for you, but they will almost certainly sell it in bags. Sometimes horses are bedded on wood chips, rather than straw. These will take longer to rot down, so in this case when you buy it it is even more important to compost it in a heap for six months to a year before using it.

Pig manure tends to be wet and cold, so not ideal for heavy soils. However, if this is all you can get it is certainly better than nothing – but in this case it is more or less essential to compost it for a year.

Chicken manure is very powerful – in all respects – but if it comes from a deep-litter farm, where it will be mixed with straw or wood chips, it is a good soil conditioner, provided it too has been composted for a year.

Geoff was a great believer in leaf mould, which he piled into a wire-netting container and consolidated by treading.

Spent mushroom compost This is usually a mixture of rotted horse manure, plus some peat (in which case Geoff would not use it) or coir, with a fairly liberal dose of lime. The lime makes it too alkaline for some soils, although mushroom growers are now removing the top layer containing the lime before selling the compost, which seems to make it fairly neutral.

Shredded prunings This is one of my own favourites. There are now a lot of good shredders on the market, which will devour your prunings and give you a wonderful fibrous mulching material. If you are thinking of buying a shredder, get the most powerful one you can afford as the smaller the shredder the longer the job will take. Geoff gave me his old shredder when he upgraded to a bigger one and I have good reason to thank the old boy every time I use it. It is so satisfying to start with a huge heap of prunings and end up with a pile of sweet-smelling chips which I know my garden will welcome. I compost mine in a heap, but Geoff used to mix his with spent potting compost before composting, to improve its quality.

Geoff looked after his worms by taking them into the greenhouse during cold weather.

Leaf mould This is the secret of really good seedbeds. Make it simply by piling all your autumn leaves into a container made from four posts driven into the ground surrounded by a piece of wire netting. Tread the leaves down hard as you fill it, because, unlike compost, leaves are broken down by fungal activity, which needs as little air as possible. In a year's time you will have a fine friable material that, if worked into the top layer of soil, will make an excellent seedbed. Geoff taught me to use leaf mould for seeds that are difficult to germinate such as parsnips. I draw a drill about 7cm (3in) deep with a swan-necked hoe and fill the drill with leaf mould, into which I sow the seed. I get 100 per cent germination every time.

Chipped bark This is used as a mulching material (see page 56) and can be bought in bags in good garden centres. It is about the same price as peat, but unlike peat it has no environmental disadvantages. It should not be dug into the soil, as it will cause nitrogen depletion. It is best left on top of the soil to rot naturally, over time.

Worm compost Geoff loved worms! I think it was a sign of a misspent youth. He swore by the product of his beloved wormery. He would sit by it at the end of the day, urging the worms on to greater and greater production. Geoff's wormery was made out of a small plastic dustbin with some holes drilled into the bottom. He also drilled a few holes into the lid for ventilation and stood the bin on a couple of bricks for drainage. Then he covered the bottom with a 5cm (2in) layer of well-rotted compost and introduced the worms — not to each other, to the compost. The best worms to use are called brandlings or manure worms, obtainable from the HDRA (the address is on page 49) as they work the compost faster and more efficiently than the common earthworm. He then added a further 15cm (6in) of compost and mixed it in with the worms. It is best, he found, to add further layers gradually, after the worms have had a chance to digest each layer of compost. The worms work most effectively at a temperature of over 15°C (60°F), so he would bring them into a garage or a heated greenhouse in the winter. When the bin was full he would sieve the contents, remove the worms and use them as the starter for the next batch. The result was a rich, crumbly material that could be used in sowing or potting composts at a ratio of about 3:1, or sprinkled in sowing drills outside to aid germination.

Green manure Green manure has been used by farmers for generations, to provide a bulky bio-mass which can easily be incorporated into the soil, lightening heavy soils, binding light soils and, in some cases, providing a source of nitrogen. Although a seemingly dying practice on farms these days it can still be a very useful and cheap way for the gardener to improve the soil. The disadvantage for gardeners is that there has to be a patch of soil available to do it and in most small gardens this is not often the case.

The secret is to use a frost-hardy bulky plant like winter grazing rye which can be grown after the vegetables have been harvested. It has a powerful root system which will help to break up and aerate the soil. Sow it in late August to late November and when you are ready to dig it in simply slice off the foliage with a sharp spade, allow it to wilt and then dig it in. Not only have you got an efficient soil conditioner for next to nothing, but you have enhanced the environment as well. Take a bow!

DIGGING IN

If your soil is heavy and difficult to work, and Geoff's was, spread a barrowload of coarse grit (at least 3mm, $\frac{1}{8}$in for us oldies), obtainable from builders' merchants or good garden centres, over every 2–3sq. yds/sq. metres of the soil you are about to dig, to give some permanent structure

Adding brandling worms to a base of compost in a home-made wormery.

to the soil when it is dug in. A layer of about 5cm (2in) will break it up and let in air. Then billions of microbes and millions of earthworms can get to work – beavering away to make your garden grow. That is a partnership worth having.

To double dig (see page 140), it is wise to dig the first trench, to a single spade's depth, at one end of the bed, load the soil into a barrow and wheel it to the other end of the bed. If you don't do this you will have a considerable levelling job to do when you have finished digging. Geoff used to tell me that one sign of a practised gardener is the ability to dig level. When the first trench is dug, the bottom should be loosened with a fork, taking care not to bring all the subsoil to the surface.

Spread a layer of organic matter – compost or manure – over the bottom of the trench, then fill it with the soil from the second trench, incorporating organic matter as you go. Give each successive trench a healthy dose of organic matter, putting it in the bottom and right up the sides to ensure that it is distributed through every level of the soil and available to roots at any stage of development. Fill the final trench with the soil you took from the first trench and, as Geoff would have said, 'The job's a good'un'.

Of course this kind of deep digging can only be done in the vegetable garden or in the initial preparation of an ornamental bed. Once the ornamental garden is established you must be careful not to disturb tender roots too much, so you should spread a thin layer of organic matter over the soil (between November and March) and then prick it over with a garden fork to bury it. Then the earthworms will do the burying work for you. This is delegation at its very best.

There is nothing more satisfying than a well-tended and productive vegetable plot, free from harmful chemicals.

RINGING THE CHANGES

Crop rotation has been practised for centuries as a means of improving soil condition and reducing pests and diseases. It has to be said that it is less relevant in the garden (and remember we can only talk about the vegetable garden here), because pests can easily travel the short distances between crops, and diseases will be carried about on your boots and your spade. Nevertheless it has a place, even if only to make your life easier. For example, it is useful to group all the heavy feeders together, particularly if you have a limited supply of manure or compost (or a bad back), so that you

YEAR 1

 A
 B
 C
 D

YEAR 2

 B
 C
 A
 D

YEAR 3

 C
 A
 B
 D

CROP ROTATION

Crops are rotated on four plots, as shown left.

A: The plot is manured and is used to grow heavy feeders such as beetroot, courgette, leek, onion, potato, shallot and tomato. Organic fertilizer (but no lime) should also be used.

B: Use organic fertilizer when the crop is sown or planted. Suitable crops are beans, chicory, lettuce, parsnip, peas, spinach, Swiss chard and sweetcorn.

C: Again, use organic fertilizer when the crop is sown or planted. Grow crops such as brassicas, radish, swede and turnip.

D: This plot contains permanent plants and is not rotated. Suitable crops are asparagus, herbs, Jerusalem artichoke, rhubarb and seakale. Apply fertilizer at least twice a year.

only have to manure that part of the garden in one year. I manure a different piece of land each year to grow my potatoes and always follow it up with crops like brassicas, which like firm land, and carrots and parsnips, which fork on over-manured land. An example of a typical crop rotation plan is shown above.

INTERCROPPING AND CATCH CROPS

In the vegetable garden it is a good idea to keep your soil covered with crops for as long as possible, because the fibrous roots of the plants will improve the soil structure and the foliage will prevent the soil from drying out. Catch crops are fast-growing crops that can be grown on bare land before it is used again. Lettuce, baby beet and radishes are examples of good catch crops. Intercropping simply means growing between rows of other vegetables that mature more slowly. For example, I grow lettuce, radish, spring onion, baby beet and baby turnips between my brassica crops – and I've usually just harvested them by the time the brassicas are expanding into the space they have taken up.

Opposite: A hose-end
applicator is an
efficient and easy way
to apply liquid fertilizer.

FERTILIZERS

The three main nutrients necessary for healthy plant growth are nitrogen, potash and phosphates. If you have conditioned your soil well these will be naturally present in the soil, but to encourage growth and replace nutrients as they are used the organic gardener may still want to use fertilizers. There are a number of trace elements that plants also need. Most of the nutrients plants need will be found in the good proprietary organic fertilizers available at garden centres or ironmongers.

Nitrogen encourages leaf growth, so it is valuable for brassicas, salad crops, spinach or any other leafy vegetable, but if you apply too much in the flower garden you will get lots of foliage and no flowers; potash helps flower and fruit formation and phosphates boost the growth of the root system. Generally you should be careful not to apply too much fertilizer because, apart from being expensive, it can scorch vulnerable roots and damage the soil structure. Stick to the instructions on the pack and don't get over enthusiastic.

Fish, blood and bone This is a reliable, balanced fertilizer, which releases potash and phosphate slowly and the nitrogen fairly fast. It's easily obtainable and cheap, so it makes a good organic standby.

Pelleted chicken manure This was one of Geoff's great favourites, because it is clean, easy to apply and has some slow-release properties. For instance, there is one available called Rooster, which comes in a bucket with a handy measure inside and instructions on how much to apply for different types of plants. It can also be mixed with water and used in liquid form and as a compost activator, so it is a very versatile product. I always have two buckets in my shed, so that as soon as one is used I can replace it with another, thus knowing I always have a stock and able to sleep easy in my bed.

Bone meal This is a phosphate fertilizer which will stimulate root growth. Spread a handful or two on the soil you have dug out of planting holes for trees or shrubs and you will help them to get off to a good start. Make sure you buy steamed bone meal, as some raw product has been known to carry the anthrax virus. Better still, play it safe by wearing rubber gloves when using it.

Wood ash If you decide to burn your prunings, rather than shred them (but remember, shredding does not damage the environment but burning does, so you should make every effort to restrict your bonfires to an absolute minimum), the ash is a useful source of potash and a little

Geoff had a dubious reputation for collecting sheep muck and making liquid fertilizer by suspending a sack of it in water.

phosphate. It is best to put it on to the compost heap, as it is highly soluble and will quickly disappear if applied directly to the soil.

Liquid fertilizers Fertilizers applied in liquid form have the great advantage of being instantly available to the plant, but the disadvantage that they leach out of the soil more quickly than other forms. They can be much cheaper but are more arduous to apply. They are usually used to give a slow-growing plant a kick in the pants or for especially gross feeders, like tomatoes or cucumbers.

I well remember the times, during the Second World War when Geoff and I were kids, being pressed into service by our dad to undertake the ignominious task of taking a bucket and collecting horse dung from the rag-and-bone man's horse, sheep droppings from the surrounding fields and cow pats from Mr Frogley's farm. We would carry them home and tip them into an evil-smelling cauldron of dark brown liquid, which we would stir up with a stick and leave to brew. We loved it. To two small boys it seemed so messy and disgusting that it had an allure all its own. When feeding time came round we would dip in the watering can and feed all our precious vegetables with it. And, by golly, did they grow!

Geoff always recommended putting the raw material into a hessian sack and suspending it in the tank of water, as this keeps the solid particles out of the water and prevents them from clogging the watering can. Use it neat on growing plants, but dilute it by 50 per cent for young seedlings to avoid scorching.

CONTROLLING PESTS AND DISEASES

The main way in which you can control pests and diseases is by not using chemicals. Look closely at a good organic garden and you will find it bustling with life – most of it friendly and productive, and working feverishly to help you to establish a garden that will give you great joy and good health by devouring pests. Birds of all kinds feed voraciously on slugs, snails and insects. Hedgehogs clean up slugs like a vacuum cleaner; ladybirds larvae dine eagerly on aphids, scale insects, mealy bugs and small caterpillars; a single hoverfly can eat fifty greenfly a day; lacewings tuck in to aphids, red spider mites, scale insects and small caterpillars – and so it goes on and on.

Remember that all predators need water. Geoff put a small pond in every organic garden he built. A pond will attract birds, insects and small mammals, who will set about your pests with enthusiasm – just like some of us, with a couple of drinks they get violent. However, Geoff was careful to point out that ponds are visited not only by wildlife. Sometimes they are visited by little children, and if this is likely they are a dangerous feature, perhaps best avoided until the kids are teenagers – by which time you will probably want to build a pond so that you can drown them yourself.

If you have a very small garden the pond could just be half a barrel, which you can get from any garden centre, sunk into the ground. Put a pile of bricks on the bottom with a stone on top, to provide a landing stage for frogs and toads and to give the birds and animals a helping hand when the water gets a bit too low for them to drink from the edge; and you can even plant it with a small aquatic plant or two, to make an attractive little feature. If you have a bigger garden you can build a more impressive water feature. Geoff recommended that the deepest part of the pond should be at least 1m (3ft) at its lowest point and then lined with sand, polythene sheeting or, best of all, a special quilt designed to prevent sharp stones puncturing the butyl liner. An alternative to a butyl liner would be a pre-formed plastic moulding, which will dispense with the need for any lining to the hole at all.

Geoff tops up his small pond to make sure his wildlife can get a drink.

Woolly aphids.

The large white butterfly, whose caterpillars feed on brassica crops.

Green aphids.

But however hungry or willing your army of predators are, you should not leave them alone to fight your battles. They can be reinforced with good growing practice as well.

THE BASIC BUILDING BLOCKS

Geoff always used to say that there are a few basic things that need to be done to provide a good start for your plants, and to minimize the risk of damage by pests and diseases. The first is to get into the habit of good cultivation practice. Nothing beats off pests and diseases like a strong healthy plant with a powerful immune system. So this means ensuring good growth by applying adequate manure and fertilizer to the soil.

Good housekeeping is particularly important. Make sure you remove dead vegetation and compost it, unless it is diseased, in which case you should burn it or make a present of it to the dustman. (Can we still call them dustmen these days?) For example, I never put old potato haulm on to my compost heap because they may be carrying potato blight spores, or fruit tree prunings, as they are likely to be carriers of mildew. Pots and seed trays should always be washed or sterilized with steam or boiling water before use.

If you are buying plants, do make certain that they are healthy. Geoff often used to show his viewers how easy it was to buy plants that are diseased, covered in pests or simply poor plants. Look carefully for signs of any pests or diseases, and for strong, vigorous growth.

Good health is just as important with plants you have raised yourself. Do not sow them too early, so that they stand in the greenhouse for too long, getting leggy and weak, and make sure that they have just the right amount of water and feed – then you will give your plants the best possible armour against pests and diseases.

USE RESISTANT VARIETIES

Geoff did not see the point of battling against nature by planting disease-prone varieties, so he advised a careful choice from the seed catalogues – not an easy task, because you may have noticed that all catalogues are written by estate agents, in glowing terms for every variety. Also if you have a persistent problem it will pay to buy varieties specifically described in the catalogue or by the garden centre as resistant to particular diseases. For example, there are few reliable organic ways to control fungal attack, such as black spot on roses, or virus diseases such as cucumber mosaic virus, but there are plenty of varieties that are resistant. Do not take resistance to mean immunity – it doesn't, but starting with resistant varieties will help you to manage your organic garden much more successfully. Remember also that F1 hybrids are generally more resistant to disease because they grow away more vigorously.

COMPANION PLANTING

Companion planting has been practised by gardeners and growers ever since Adam made his fatal mistake and was obliged to get down to some real gardening. It is based on the theory that weeds and pests can be reduced by selective planting. For example, weeds can be kept down by planting low, spreading plants between tall ones; the cabbage white butterfly, which is attracted by smell, can be misled by planting the pungent French marigold (*Tagetes*) between brassica rows. But be warned: there is a lot of folklore attached to companion planting and its success has not been conclusively proved, so it should never be your sole defence. For instance, some people claim that planting carrots next to onions defeats carrot fly, because they too are attracted by smell and the strong smell of the onions obscures the smell of the carrot, but I have never found this to be the case. Geoff was always a bit circumspect about companion planting. He would have loved all the old folklore to be true, but his trials had not convinced him by any means, except for the use of French marigolds to deter the cabbage white. He also believed in the invaluable use of flowers to attract predators and hide vegetable crops. French marigolds, which attract hoverfly, whose larvae feed greedily on aphids, and so are useful planted close to tomatoes or roses; poppies, nasturtiums and morning glory do the same, and all provide you with a colourful display as well. Vegetables hidden in the flower border will escape attack simply because it is harder for the pests to find them, especially if they are planted singly.

OTHER WAYS OF CONTROLLING PESTS AND DISEASES

In addition to all the methods I have described, there are other organic methods of dealing with particular pests and diseases. The charts on pages 50–53 suggest ways of handling those you are most likely to come up against. If you have a persistent problem or one not covered here, try contacting the HDRA: the Organic Organisation, Ryton Organic Gardens, Ryton-on-Dunsmore, Coventry CV8 3LG.

PEST AND DISEASE CONTROL

There are, of course, an awful lot of pests and diseases, so I shall deal only with the ways of handling those you are most likely to come up against. Pests really fall into three categories - birds and animals, soil borne pests and other. I have summarized the control methods for the more common pests and diseases in the following tables.

Vine weevils.

Leatherjackets.

Controlling flea beetle with a piece of grease-coated wood.

PEST	WHAT THEY ATTACK	CONTROL
BIRDS AND ANIMALS		
Birds	Almost any plant, especially brassicas. Birds can completely destroy leafy crops, damage seedlings and uproot onion sets	Wire netting hoops for seedlings Netting for bigger plants Horticultural fleece
Deer (can be a menace in the country)	All vegetation and the bark of trees	Electric fencing, installed by an expert
Rabbits	All vegetation	Wire netting fencing buried 5cm (2in) with a further 10cm (4 in) curving out from the base of the fence
Moles	Lawns and borders	Humane barrel trap
SOIL-BORNE PESTS		
Leatherjackets	Lawns, brassicas, lettuce strawberries and ornamental plants especially when young	Cover the ground with black plastic at night. Pick up the leatherjackets in the morning
Slugs	All root crops and most leafy crops, making holes in leaves and often stripping them	Pick up at night and drop into paraffin Surround vulnerable plants with soot, lime or pine bark Cover vulnerable plants with a plastic bottle with the top cut off. Use nematodes as a biological control
Cutworms	Young plants, eating them off at the base	Keep weeds down and the ground clean to remove their habitat Cultivate often in winter to expose caterpillars to predators and the weather Protect vulnerable plants with plastic bottles or toilet roll tubes Vigilance. Pick up cutworms around damaged plants
Ants	Ants undermine roots of young plants	Cold, or boiling water to wash the nest away
OTHER PESTS		
Aphids (greenfly and blackfly)	Roses, lupins, broad beans and many greenhouse and other plants – aphids feed of the soft tissue of the plant and suck the sap, secreting a sticky honeydew	Encourage predators by planting *Tagetes* Cover vegetables with horticultural fleece Pick off aphids early and cut out and destroy infested shoots Use a strong jet of cold water to dislodge them Pinch out top shoots of broad beans as soon as infestation appears In the greenhouse use the biological control *Aphidius* Insecticidal soap or derris as a last resort
Woolly aphid	Apples, crab apple, cotoneaster, hawthorn, pyracantha, sorbus and other plants – the aphid produces a fluffy outgrowth on plant stems and tree branches	Encourage predators by planting any member of the *Compositae* or *Umbelliferae* families or the poached egg plant or convolvulus Prune out and burn severely affected branches As a last resort spray several times with insecticidal soap
Earwigs	Dahlias, chrysanthemums and other flowering plants – flowers are distorted and misshapen	Fill a flowerpot with grass and invert it on a cane near the flower head. The earwigs will crawl in and once a week the grass can be burnt
Woodlice	Roots and stems of many young plants are eaten off at the base	Good housekeeping – they live under garden debris Regular cultivation to expose them to predators Entice them under a plate with a cheese or potato bait and then pick them up in the morning. Put a band of grease round the legs of greenhouse staging

PEST	WHAT THEY ATTACK	CONTROL
Caterpillars	Brassicas, fruit, flowering plants and many other vegetables – holes appear in the leaves and they can be completely stripped	Hand pick them and drop them into a jar of paraffin. Rub eggs off by hand Use the biological control *Bacillus thuringiensis* Use derris as a last resort
Cabbage root fly	All brassicas – the adult lays its eggs at the base of the plant and the larvae cause the plant to collapse	Surround the plant stem with 15cm (6in) squares of carpet underlay or buy cabbage stem guards
Onion fly	Onions and other bulbs – grubs attack the roots and plants yellow and die in midsummer	Hoe regularly to expose the grubs to birds Grow multi-sown blocks in the greenhouse or use sets
Carrot fly	Carrots, parsnips, parsley and celery – grubs burrow into the root and cause brown discoloration and tunnels	Select a windswept site if possible as the fly likes shelter Use resistant varieties – e.g. Sytan Avoid sowing at egg laying time – May and August Sow thinly to avoid the need for thinning which attracts the adult Use a non-woven fleece Erect a low polythene barrier round the crop – the fly will miss it
Pea moth, codling moth and plum moth	The grub will enter the pea pod and attack the pea, making it inedible. It will cause similar damage in apples and plums	Cover peas with fleece Use the biological sex attractant, pheromones. This is contained in a trap which will lure the moth to the bait Use derris as a last resort
Whitefly	Brassicas and many greenhouse plants – they suck the sap, but healthy plants can withstand quite severe attacks	Remove infected leaves before 'scales' become adults Use a battery powered hoover on the adults (if you think it's worth it) Hose down with a good jet of cold water In the greenhouse, hang up a yellow card coated with grease In the greenhouse use the biological control *Encarsia*
Vine weevil	Usually container-grown plants. Also fuchsia, primula, cyclamen and begonia	Vigilance. Knock newly bought plants out of their pots to inspect.. Biological control, using a nematode *Heterohabditis megidis*. As a last resort dip the whole pot into a solution of derris
Flea beetle	Brassicas, radishes, turnips, mustard and other cruciferous plants – the beetle eats small holes in the leaf, which can check growth and kill young plants	Coat a piece of wood with heavy grease and pass it along the row of plants. The insects will jump up and stick to the grease. Cover with horticultural fleece as soon as seed is sown Clear accumulated debris to remove overwintering environment
Red spider mite	A wide range of greenhouse plants – the mite sucks the sap and can kill the plants It can also be a problem outside in dry years	Spray with water regularly, as the mite likes dry conditions Use the biological control *Phytoseiulus*, a predatory mite
Sciarid fly (fungus fly)	A greenhouse and houseplant pest which nibbles off the stem of the plant, just below ground level	Cover the surface of pot plants with horticultural sand or grit Reduce watering to a minimum Hang yellow card, coated with grease near the plant Use one of the biological controls, *Hypoaspis miles*, a mite or *Steinernema feltiae*, a nematode

DISEASE	WHAT IT ATTACKS	CONTROL
Club root	All brassicas — caused by a soil-borne fungus which distorts and thickens the root and causes stunting or failure	There is no cure for club root. Alleviate the effects by raising plants in pots Rotate crops regularly Lime your soil frequently up to pH 7.5 Grow resistant varieties
Potato blight	Potatoes – starts with brown patches on the leaves and finally reduces the crop to a brown, stinking mess. Occurs in warm, wet weather	Spray with Bordeaux mixture fortnightly from July If blight strikes cut down all the foliage and harvest three weeks later Burn all potato haulm
Rose black spot	Roses – appears as dark spots on the leaves. Leaves can fall and leaf buds die back	Grow resistant varieties Provide good growing conditions but reduce nitrogen
Botryitis	Most common disease of greenhouse and outdoor plants. Causes brown spots or blotches followed by grey mould	Good air circulation Beware of damaging seedlings Fertilize and water sparingly Avoid planting in shady, damp spots
Apple scab	Apples and pears – fruit becomes blotched with corky patches. The fruit may split but will not rot	Buy resistant varieties Cut out and burn affected twigs Ignore it — it doesn't affect the taste
Potato blackleg	Potatoes – this is a bacterial disease that causes the stems to blacken and die. Tubers can also be affected	Burn all affected haulm Never store affected tubers Buy resistant varieties
Onion neck rot	Onions – symptoms appear in store. Upper part of the bulb is soft and the rot spreads down the bulb	Rotation, for as long as possible Do not overfeed Don't bend tops over to ripen
Onion white rot	Onions, leeks, garlic, chives, shallots and spring onions – white, fluffy growths appear on roots and plants die	Rotation, for as long as possible Treat with Bordeaux mixture Very difficult to control
Mildews	Most fruit, begonias, poppies, rose, most young shoots in garden and greenhouse	Increase air circulation in greenhouse Feed sparingly Keep the soil or compost moist Burn infected leaves As a last resort spray with copper fungicide or dispersible sulphur
Damping off	A greenhouse disease which causes seedlings to blacken and rot at the stem	Sow thinly. Reduce watering. Increase greenhouse temperature. As a last resort, water with copper fungicide
Chocolate spot	Broad beans – brown spots form, sometimes joining up and killing the plant	Adequate feeding and mulching As a last resort spray with copper fungicide
Potato scab	Potatoes – forms corky patches on the outside of the tubers	Incorporate plenty of organic matter Use resistant varieties Water well in dry spells
Spraing	Potatoes – causes brown, semi-circular lesions on the inside of the tuber	Use resistant varieties Long rotation periods No other cure
Parsnip canker	Parsnips – causes reddish marks at the crown, which may spread	Grow resistant varieties

DISEASE	WHAT IT ATTACKS	CONTROL
Bacterial canker	Plums – causes holes in leaves at first, followed by a sticky secretion from the branches	Cut away and burn all infected wood As a last resort spray with copper fungicide once a month for three months from mid-summer
Peach leaf curl	All prunus species – red blisters appear on leaves and they turn white and fall early, reducing the vigour of the tree	Remove infected leaves Spray with copper fungicide at least twice in winter and repeat in autumn Protect trees from rain, which carries spores
Fireblight (a notifiable disease)	Apples, pears and ornamental trees in the *Rosaceae* family. Infected shoots turn brown and cankers develop at the base of the shoot	Notify the Ministry of Agriculture Cut out the diseased wood 2–3ft below the infection or burn the whole tree

Late blight on potato plant.

Blackspot on rose bush.

Botrytis cinerea on chrysanthemum house plant.

Powdery mildew on *Achillea ptarmica* 'The Pearl'.

Opposite: Geoff mulches his borders with his fine, crumbly compost.

CONTROLLING WEEDS

In the organic garden it is not an acceptable practice to use any chemical herbicides at all. Of course with some weeds, such as ground elder, bindweed or couch grass, that are difficult to control the temptation to reach for the bottle is very great. However, there are alternative solutions that have no harmful effect on soil organisms, birds, mammals, insects or people.

WEED-FREE LAWNS

There are really only three ways I know to keep your lawn weed-free organically. The first is regular mowing. This will quickly destroy taller weeds and will also strengthen your grass, so that it is better able to compete with weeds. The second is to put a tiny pinch of salt on to the weeds, which will then die. Take care not to get the salt on the grass or that will die also. The third and most effective way to remove weeds is to dig them out with a knife or one of the special tools that can be bought from garden centres. This is quite a time-consuming job but at least by removing them this way you will have the satisfaction of knowing that you have done so properly – and the job will get easier every year.

CLEANING CROPS

For a new garden or a weed-infested vegetable garden a crop like potatoes will do a lot to rid you of the weeds. It is cultivated three times – once when you dig and set the seed, next when you earth up and finally when you harvest – and each time the weeds will take a battering. The foliage will eventually meet between the rows and it will be dense enough to deprive weeds of the light they need to grow. But beware: this is not true of climbing weeds such as bindweed, which seem to find their way to the light in any conditions.

MULCHING

All plants need light to grow and if you exclude it with a mulch they will eventually give up the fight. Some of the more laid-back gurus recommend old carpet for this job, but unless you want your garden to look like a division of Allied Carpets, I would avoid it. You certainly wouldn't see a piece of carpet in one of Geoff's gardens. Instead he would use one of the following methods.

Black polythene Black polythene does the same job as carpet, but it can look pretty unsightly on its own. However, if you lay the polythene on the soil, bury the edges in a shallow trench or hold it down with stones or soil,

and then plant through it, by making small slits in the polythene to accommodate the plant, when the plants have grown you will not see the polythene at all. If you have an area more than 1.2 m (4ft) wide you will need to lay a length of seep hose underneath so that the plants are adequately watered. Alternatively you can spread shredded bark or gravel on top of the polythene to hide it.

Compost As well as making a good mulch to retain moisture and provide some nutrients, compost can be used to suppress weed growth, but be sure you apply a very heavy layer and remember that it may contain weed seeds.

Bark A 7cm (3in) layer of shredded or chopped bark is an excellent weed suppressant. The initial outlay is high but it will last several years.

Gravel It is very fashionable to use gravel these days, and it is a very effective inhibitor of weeds. It also looks attractive in the right setting. However, it will not suppress the more tenacious perennial weeds and it makes it difficult to hoe them out. If you put some polypropylene ground cover sheet under the gravel you should have no trouble.

Grass cuttings Fresh grass cuttings can be used as a weed-suppressing mulch. They are not very attractive after a few days, and they should not be laid too thickly as this will exclude air from the bottom layers and you will be left with a slimy mess. But they can be useful in an appropriate setting. I use them around the fruit trees in an orchard next to my garden, which I mow for a blind lady in the village. I lay them on thickly and end up with a circle of clear soil around the base of the tree that I can't get to with the mower.

GROUND COVER

Strong healthy plants are probably the best weed suppressant of all, but you must start with a clean piece of land so that they do not have weed competition in the early stages. Many flowering plants will self-seed if the seed heads are not removed too soon and two or three years after planting up a new border you will have a dense covering of foliage, which will fight off the weeds. Then you will have a virtually weed-free garden and you will only need to remove the more invasive plants, or those that are out of place for your taste. We have a couple of borders that are weeded only once a year – after the forget-me-nots have flowered – and are a delight to see.

There are many spreading plants which will quickly cover the ground, but do take great care not to plant anything that is so vigorous that it will

Black polythene sheet used as a mulch between rows of runner beans.

quickly eat you out of house and home, like *Viola riviniana* Purpurea Group (syn. *V. labradorica* 'Purpurea') or comfrey, *Symphytum grandiflorum*. I have both these plants in my own garden and, having lovingly planted them, I spend a good part of my life pulling them out again. Either plant would be OK in the right place — a woodland garden or a wild garden — but that isn't where I have them. So look up ground cover plants before you buy and ask the advice of the nurseryman.

Geoff found that a wheel hoe was one of the most useful tools with which to hoe down his vegetable rows.

HOEING

Regular hoeing is your most effective weapon against weeds, and it is easy if you do it regularly. Hoe in dry weather if possible, when they are easily loosened from the soil, or else you will simply transplant the weeds. I make a practice of hoeing routinely even if there are no weeds to be seen, because pulling the hoe through the soil will disturb and kill all the weeds that are germinating just below the soil surface. If the weather is dry, leave the weeds where they are so that they will rot down and give some organic matter back to the soil; if it's wet, remove them, or else they will root back into the soil. If you live in Manchester or we have one of our normal wet summers, you will just have to remove the weeds as you go (sorry Manchester, that was cruel).

LOOKING FOR TROUBLE

Geoff once told me of an elderly organic gardener he interviewed for one of his programmes — a Yorkshireman, I believe. Geoff asked him, 'How do you manage to keep your garden so free of pests and diseases?' With a straight face he replied, 'I do a lot o' lookin'!' If you hoe your garden regularly as you see weeds appear you will keep the weeds at bay before they have any effect at all on the surrounding plants. If you see a sign of mildew you can catch it in its early stages: just pull off the leaf and dispose of it. Caterpillars can be picked off easily when young and aphids can be killed when they first attack simply by rubbing them with your fingers to squash them. It takes a little time but it is well worth the bother. Geoff and Lynda used to stroll round the gardens at Barnsdale together every evening and I do exactly the same with my wife. With two sets of eyes on the lookout we don't miss much. Geoff's Yorkshireman put his finger on the secret of good organic gardening.

The great peat crusade

THE ROAD TO DAMASCUS

From the first time our father showed him how to use peat to make a first-rate growing medium for his beloved chrysanthemums, Geoff was a peat enthusiast. In the early years of his career he wrote about peat, enthused about peat on television, and advised endlessly on the use of peat. Peat was in his blood, as well as under his fingernails and in his boots.

He heard a few murmurings from growers and horticultural scientists to the effect that peat was an overrated growing medium, and from some environmentalists who were beginning to suggest that the use of peat was damaging wildlife habitats. He even had letters from viewers complaining about his advocacy of peat. But Geoff had always used it satisfactorily and he had certainly never seen any environmental damage.

So in typically positive style he decided to take a trip to Ireland to see for himself. He was excited and interested at the prospect of seeing peat production at first hand and arranged an invitation from the Irish Peat Board, the Bórd na Móna, to see one of the many peat bogs that abound in Ireland. He was greeted by one of their representatives and together they left the city, travelling through the suburbs until, quite suddenly, they found themselves in a wild and lonely area of wilderness. The bog lands of Ireland are a mysterious blend of great beauty and harsh weather where, though the rain seems to fall incessantly and the wind soughs across the land, there is a vibrant abundance of wildlife. Skylarks, curlew, meadow pipits and heron fill the air with sights and sound and bog cotton, ling heather and the delicate yellow bog asphodel flourish.

There in this wild place they stopped to watch a sight that made Geoff grin with delight. An old man was cutting peat for his fire with a spade – one of the spades specially designed for the job many hundreds of years ago. He was loading it on to a cart, drawn by a patient donkey. Geoff had always, since his early days of working in nurseries, maintained a deep respect for the working man. He worked extremely hard himself and he had learned the dignity of work and how it can, given the right conditions, elevate the spirit. In particular he was inspired by the idea of working in harmony with one's environment so that you and your natural resources work together to preserve and sustain each other. So the idea of people drawing their warmth from the land without damaging it seemed to him deeply satisfying. He was not sentimental about this; he knew that most people can not live that way – that most have to live in the town or city.

An example of the damage that is being done daily to the last remaining raised peat bogs in Britain.

But that knowledge was what inspired his work. The thought that he could do something to help people keep in touch with nature and the wild environment was the source of all his enthusiasm for his job.

He chatted briefly with the peat cutter; then he returned to his Land Rover and they drove on.

And that was when it happened.

As they rounded a bend and dropped down into a dip in the moors they came upon a huge, hungry machine, ripping and tearing its way through the peat with a ferocity Geoff could hardly believe. Vast quantities of peat were being loaded on to trailers. This was a delicate environment that gave life to rare plants and animals, such as the insect-eating sundew and even the nightjar, and this monster was removing them and their entire habitat with precision efficiency. What was left was a desolate moonscape of rutted mud that would never recover.

Geoff could only stand and look, dumbstruck. As if from far away, he heard the man from the Irish Peat Board telling him statistics. He talked not about the destruction but about the income it generated. He talked about the value of peat to gardeners and commercial growers, and even about the fact that it is burned in power stations. Geoff was speechless.

Once on the ferry home he settled gratefully into the bar, ordered himself a beer and thought about the day. Everything he stood for he had just seen disappearing into the jaws of a mighty machine, apparently so that gardeners could pretty up their gardens. Hammering inside his head was the thought that, through his television programmes and his writing, he was actually helping to promote this wanton destruction – the very opposite of his ideal of living in harmony with nature. A sombre mood settled over him as he considered the power of the great companies who sell and promote the use of peat, and how well established the use of peat was with the public.

But Geoff was always a fighter and his mood of despondency did not last long. Before he had finished his beer he was planning a fight-back.

First he would need to do some research to make sure that gardeners were indeed contributing to what he had just seen. If they were, he had to discover a way to persuade them not to do it. To do this he would need to find an alternative to peat that was as good, as cheap and as convenient. He knew that work was already being done in this area, and if he could persuade gardeners to stop using peat, this might persuade the other invaders to relent. He fished for his notebook and began to make plans – for trials he could carry out at Barnsdale, for making contact with people with a common cause, even the outline of an article for the gardening press. By the time he rolled off the ferry he was ready for a campaign.

THE TRIALS AND THE TRIBULATIONS

At 8.00 a.m. on the morning of the day after his return from Ireland Geoff was in his office, sleeves rolled up. His first task was to find out the extent of the problem and what work had already been done to try to prevent it. So he got in touch with Friends of the Earth, Professor David Bellamy, Plantlife, English Nature, the Wildlife Commission and a host of others who had an interest in preserving this unique habitat.

A mechanical peat mill tearing the heart out of one of the few surviving peat bogs.

At the end of that morning's work he had a notepad full of facts and a head full of ideas and aspirations. The rate of peat depletion was alarming, although it was perhaps least worrying in the Irish Republic, where he had first seen the problem, because it had the largest reserves. The fact was that Ireland used to have 770,000 acres of raised bog and was now down to its last 50,000 acres. All over Britain and Ireland raised peat bogs, so called because of their distinctive dome-shaped topography, were being subjected not only to peat cutting for burning both in power stations and domestically and for horticulture but also to damage through opencast mining, forestry and building. Peat was even being used as litter for racehorses. He discovered that peat bogs such as Thorne and Hatfield Moors in South Yorkshire and Wedholme Flow in Cumbria, both Sites of Special Scientific Interest, and which give life to over 2,000 wildlife species, were disappearing at high speed. He also learned from Dr Jane Smart,

Top: Drosera intermedia growing in boggy ground near Trudernish, near Ardtalla, East Islay.

Above: Scarlet elf cup (*Sarcoscypha coccinea*) in a peat bog in Yorkshire.

director of Plantlife, that peat removal was contributing to the depletion of the ozone layer. 'These bogs are a huge carbon store,' she said, 'full of lots of "pickled plants". Once you start to mess up the surface these start to break down and release massive amounts of carbon dioxide into the atmosphere.' Dr Smart also talked about attempts to reclaim worked-out bog lands. She said, 'I wish to make it abundantly clear that all the work in this area has failed to show that it is possible to return the bog to its natural pristine condition, at least within a meaningful time frame. And the cost of peatland rehabilitation is astronomical.'

Geoff had no doubt that some of the blame for all this damage could be laid at the doors of innocent gardeners. But he now knew he had some allies; and he also knew that he could make a significant contribution to the search for an alternative. His next task was to map out a series of trials to demonstrate the way plants responded to different media, which he would show to his viewers. He worked on that day in a fury of activity, forgetting his lunch, inspired by his ideas but also angry at the way in which the countryside was being ravaged in pursuit of commercial gain. By the time he was called for his dinner, in the late evening, he realized that the task ahead of him was challenging but not insuperable – and that he was ravenously hungry. But on his desk lay a plan that was to prove to be exciting and deeply fulfilling.

That night he wrestled with the facts he had learned. Peat was providing cheap fuel for power stations, and who could deny that cheap fuel was desirable? Domestic peat cutting was still taking large quantities but declining. Horticultural peat represented a rapidly growing but nevertheless relatively small proportion of the total degradation of the peat bogs. Maybe all this destruction could to some extent be justified and was not worth worrying about. But at what cost? Could we really justify the elimination of the rare nightjar, the bee orchid and the timid Irish hare? Were we anxious to promote the destruction of the magnificent scarlet elf cup, the large heath butterfly or even the humble dor beetle? Could we live with the fact that only 6 per cent of the UK's raised bogs are left? As Geoff was to write in a *Gardeners' World* publication, 'Huge milling machines rip up vast quantities of peat, removing, according to one estimate, 1.76 million cubic metres per year. That is enough to comfortably fill the National Exhibition Centre in Birmingham and still have some left over for growing bags. It is estimated that there are less than 3000 hectares of natural, untouched peat bog left in Britain – an area about the size of Brighton.' The more he reflected on what he had unearthed the more convinced he became that he should proceed with his plan.

He knew that whatever he did in his trials had to be fair and scientifically controlled, so he decided that every one would run alongside a peat alternative. They would receive exactly the same conditions of sowing, watering, feeding, heat and light, so that an exact comparison could be made. He knew he had to be beyond criticism if his arguments were to be effective.

Peat has been a mainstay of soil conditioning and propagation for many years and its popularity has been increased by the fact that its rich brown or black colour gives an impression of fertility. This is entirely untrue. In fact, peat, like coir, is a completely sterile medium with no fertile properties at all. The fact that it absorbs about five times its weight in water seems good to gardeners working on drier, sandy soils, but the truth is that this property simply has the effect of surrounding the plant roots with a cold sticky mass which can inhibit rather than enhance growth. It also has a very open texture, which gives the impression that it is a good soil conditioner, but there is considerable doubt about this also. Geoff discovered during his researches that a series of trials run by the Department of Transport, which plants millions of trees, shrubs and herbaceous plants every year, showed that in most cases the use of peat either made no difference at all or actually inhibited growth. Therefore as a soil conditioner it seemed to be of little value but there was no doubt that, if mixed with other ingredients and properly fed it was a first-class medium for seed sowing, propagation and for growing plants on, so this was going to be a hard nut to crack.

Geoff's early trials were about the propagation of plants, with seeds and cuttings. With convenience for the gardener in mind he began with germination trials in the greenhouse, using readily available materials. He tried garden compost, leaf mould, chopped straw and spent mushroom compost, as well as a range of commercial peat-free products that were beginning to find their way on to the market.

He found that garden compost was too variable in nutrients for proper control; leaf mould exposed seedlings to fungal attack; chopped straw, whilst moderately good as a sowing medium, gave poor results when seedlings were pricked out into it; and mushroom compost was far too alkaline.

Some of the commercial peat-free products he tried were as good as peat, but he could not honestly say that any were better. This worried him because he knew that if he was to convince his viewers and readers he had

Coconut husks in Sri Lanka being converted into fibre.

to be able to offer something that would exceed their current expectations. Who was going to change to a new growing medium for their precious plants if there was no evidence that the results were better?

But all the time his trials were in progress he was keeping his ear to the ground about new products and what others were doing to advance the cause – and it was in this way that he discovered coir.

THE COIR STORY

Coir, most of which comes to this country from Sri Lanka, is a waste product of the coconut fibre industry. Coconut fibre, which is removed from the husks of coconuts, is used for making ropes, brushes and doormats, and in the upholstery trade. What is left behind is a large amount of a fine material called pith. This is stacked in huge heaps and weathered for a number of years. What is now coir is then dried and formed into bricks for transport. Once it arrives in this country the coir is rewetted and bagged for sale to gardeners, or delivered in bulk to commercial growers. It is subject to rigorous quality control by the Sri Lankan universities, specialists in the factories, the Ministry of Agriculture in the UK and the coir compost producers, who have set up intensive systems to ensure extremely high standards of quality, chemical composition and hygiene. In fact, it has been found that coir is less infected with harmful microorganisms than ordinary garden soil.

The early trials Geoff carried out with coir, with seeds and cuttings, were not highly successful. He found that it tended to dry out very quickly and that plant growth was not as vigorous as when he used a peat-based compost. He struggled and worried and schemed about why this was – then suddenly it came to him. Because coir looked like peat he was treating it like peat. But coir is different. It is much more open and free draining, and because of this it is more likely to dry out. When the top of the coir looks dry it is tempting to water it, and as the water runs through the open coir it takes all the added nutrients with it, which results in spindly growth.

So what was the answer? First he tried watering and feeding more often, but this was time-consuming and expensive, especially as he had over 150,000 perennials and shrubs to look after, in 1,000 different varieties. He would have been exhausted and bankrupted if he'd continued with that. But a little thought and research amongst commercial growers brought a rich reward. The answer was to set up a capillary system, so that the plants were watered from the bottom.

He covered his slatted greenhouse staging with outdoor quality plywood which had been wrapped in a sheet of polythene. Then he laid a sheet of capillary matting, bought from the local garden centre, on the polythene and set his pots on top. Then it was simply a matter of watering the matting, rather than the pot — much quicker and easier. It was important to ensure that the staging was level, so that the water did not run off. When you water this way the water is drawn up into the pot, partly by capillary action and partly by pressure exerted by the plant's roots. Overhead watering can then be done only occasionally. Even though it may look as though the top has dried out, in most cases a little investigation into the lower levels of the compost with the tips of the fingers will show that the pot is moist further down — where it matters.

Of course it is not necessarily easy or possible for everybody to use capillary matting. You might not have a greenhouse and even if you do you might find it difficult to get the greenhouse staging exactly level. But if capillary matting is not a practical proposition it is still possible to use

Processing coconut fibre into coir compost for export from Sri Lanka.

One of Geoff's coir compost trials in progress.

coir as an alternative to peat; it is just necessary to water coir more often — say every five days instead of every seven.

Clearly it was then important to introduce a regular regime of feeding, starting about four weeks after sowing and three weeks after potting. Geoff found it was best to use a slow-release fertilizer, either in pellet or liquid form, or it is possible to get the same results by feeding more often than you would when using peat — say once more every four or five weeks. Feeding would also of course be necessary for house plants grown in coir indoors.

The Barnsdale trials also took into account the fact that not all amateur gardeners get it right. Geoff knew that he had to allow for those of his viewers and readers who were fairly new to the game. So he tried replicating the two most common amateur mistakes: sowing too deeply and overwatering. He was delighted to find that coir responded well to both these problems, producing plants that were just as good as those that had been sown with his expert knowledge — and much better than those that had been sown in peat.

However, he did find that he needed practice before he got the watering and feeding exactly right. But with a little patience and his natural feel for plants he was soon producing specimens that stood proudly beside peat-grown plants, looking stronger and healthier, and, using a capillary system of watering and slow-release fertilizer, with less watering and feeding effort.

As a result of the trials Geoff decided there and then to change the whole propagation policy of Barnsdale and the small commercial nursery that he had set up shortly after coming to Barnsdale. He decided to grow all his plants in coir. This is a policy which continues to this day, under the management of his son Nick and Nick's wife Sue, and the nursery stock and the gardens at Barnsdale are a testament to its success.

THE CAMPAIGN BEGINS

With all the experience and knowledge he had gained during his researches into peat and its alternatives Geoff was keen to broadcast and write about his views and findings. Knowing that he would get a less than enthusiastic welcome from the peat industry, he was cautious but he was not daunted, as he was a hardened journalist by now and only the justice and good sense of his mission concerned him. So he began to write and broadcast the facts about the use of peat and its devastating effect on the raised bogs of the UK, and he never lost an opportunity to advise gardeners that for all greenhouse applications, containers, hanging baskets, etc. coir was a better option and for soil conditioning there was a whole range of better and cheaper organic options. He had always believed in the good sense and selflessness of the average gardener; he just thought they had not been told the facts – after all, he had only recently become aware of the problem himself, even though he was at the forefront of knowledge about horticultural practice – and he felt that once they knew the facts gardeners would want to be working with, rather than against, nature.

His campaign was not always without its difficulties. Almost before it had started the chairman of the Peat Producers Association sent a letter to the Director General of the BBC, complaining that Geoff was biased and alleging that his facts were inaccurate. The letter stopped short of asking for the death penalty, but it was highly critical.

To the credit of the BBC, its reply explained and verified the facts that Geoff had quoted on *Gardeners' World*. Against the charge of bias, it pointed out that not only had Peter Seabrook, a distinguished horticultural broadcaster, been given an opportunity to counter Geoff's views, but two other experts had presented opposing views. The reply said the BBC would stand by Geoff and continue to support his work.

He also had a run-in with the Consumers' Association about its stand at the Chelsea Flower Show, which compared coir unfavourably with peat. Geoff wrote an article which claimed that the results displayed at Chelsea were unscientific, as the underlying trials had failed to test each medium under the optimal conditions required for it. In other words, peat was bound to win because coir had been nobbled from the start. This dispute was resolved with the subsequent publication of a clarifying statement in *Gardeners' World* magazine which explained Geoff's contention that coir must be treated differently from peat and the correct treatment had not been demonstrated at Chelsea.

But despite such brickbats Geoff was spurred on by the fact that he began to sense growing interest in and approval of his views from his audience. After every programme he broadcast and every article he wrote about the good sense of substituting coir for peat he was inundated with letters, telephone calls, faxes and e-mails expressing support – like this letter he received from a lady in Ipswich:

Strong, sturdy seedlings growing in modules in coir compost.

Opposite: The luxuriant
growth in these
hanging baskets at
Barnsdale clearly
demonstrates the
success of growing in
coir.

Dear Mr Hamilton,

I would like to congratulate you on your campaign against peat use — bringing the fate of Britain's peat bogs to the attention of Britain's gardeners in such a committed way. Most people don't want a heather bed at the expense of a natural area of beauty — they just don't know what is going on to provide the product. Your practical research into alternatives, your straightforward, 'non-cranky' approach and determination to mention the subject whenever possible have, in my opinion, done more to save the peat bogs than any other campaign.

Well done, Mr Hamilton, and thank you.

Such support encouraged him to continue his campaign, and in 1991 he spoke at a Commission of Enquiry into Peat and Peatlands, organized by Plantlife and supported by English Nature, the Joint Nature Conservation Committee and the World Wide Fund for Nature. He presented the case for coir with Neil Bragg of ADAS (the government's Agricultural Development and Advisory Service). Together they gave a balanced and fair assessment of the relative merits of the two materials, but they both came down in favour of peat-free composts, both for technical and for environmental reasons.

Of course Geoff was not the only person researching and campaigning for the use of peat-free composts; there were trials being done by ten other groups, including Friends of the Earth. But it was probably Geoff's voice that was heard most often, because through television and journalism he had direct access to gardeners and, through them, to commercial growers and retailers.

So what did the campaign achieve? The first major breakthrough came with the Peat Protection Charter, which asks all local authorities to use peat alternatives and to encourage individual gardeners and growers to do the same. It was launched by the Prince of Wales, who said:

The use of peat in gardening and landscaping schemes seems to me to be causing the quite unnecessary destruction of a richly varied and scarce wildlife habitat ... If we would like other countries to stop regarding their rainforests as 'useless jungle', we would do well to set an example by not treating our peatland habitat as 'useless bog' ... I have therefore decided to stop using peat on my garden at Highgrove and contracts for landscaping schemes for the Duchy of Cornwall will now specify that peat is not to be used.

This was powerful support indeed. The charter, and the anti-peat

This greenhouse at Barnsdale must surely dispel any doubts about the value of coir as a growing medium.

campaigning in which Geoff's own work played a leading role, succeeded in increasing public awareness both of the environmental effects of using peat and of the benefit of using coir, with significant results.

An RSPB survey in 1994 showed that all forty-six county councils in England and Wales and seven regional councils in Scotland were now using peat alternatives. The Royal Botanic Gardens at Kew, London, now uses no peat at all and grows many thousands of plants of all kinds successfully in coir composts. Many large commercial growers use coir to grow hundreds of thousands of plants successfully. One very large grower told Geoff that he was not interested in saving peat bogs, but he would not go back to growing in peat for a pension because his results with coir were so much better.

The first retailers to stop selling peat-based composts from Sites of Special Scientific Interest (SSSI) were B&Q and they were quickly followed by Do It All, Great Mills and Homebase, who collectively have the lion's share of the garden compost market.

Unfortunately the battle is not yet won. There is still massive despoliation of the raised bogs and although during the height of Geoff's television and press campaign to help save the peat bogs the sales of peat dropped dramatically, now that such pressure is no longer being applied they are beginning to creep up again.

So why are more gardeners not using coir? As Geoff reported to the 1991 Commission of Enquiry, it is partly because gardeners have simply become used to buying peat. It's clean and light and you can just pick it up in a plastic bag in any garden centre. Coir, although it is also clean, light and can be picked up in a plastic bag, is not stocked by all garden centres, because people are simply not asking for it, although this is becoming less and less the case, as gardeners are becoming more aware of the damage peat extraction is doing.

The second reason is cost. At the moment peat is about 30 per cent cheaper to buy than coir. Why? John Bruce, a director of Coir Ltd, the biggest importer of coir for horticulture in this country, says that the actual cost of the material in a 70-litre (15-gallon) bag of coir, after production, baling and transport to the UK, is just 58p. All the other costs – bagging, quality control, distribution, etc. – are the same as for peat. The actual cost of a cubic metre of peat in 1998 was £35 while a cubic metre of coir cost £19. The reason coir is priced higher is simply that at present it is a so-called niche product, so retailers put a higher price tag on it. It is time this stopped, and only we gardeners can stop it – by buying more so that retailers will no longer be able to argue that it is a niche product and will be obliged to bring the price down, while making it well known that we know we are being cheated.

Reiterating Geoff's findings, Mr Bruce also says that coir is a proven alternative to peat, worldwide; it is physically and chemically a better product than most peats. Yet at present it represents only 3–4 per cent of the market. Surely, given the known damage to the environment by the use of peat and the known benefits of coir, major wholesale buyers should be demanding that plants are grown peat free and the large garden centres and DIY chains should be encouraging the use of coir and selling it at fair and sensible prices?

So come on, gardeners of the world, unite. Let us put our weight behind the campaign that Geoff fought so hard for and ensure that he did not fight in vain.

People who live in glass houses

THE GLASSY STAIR

One of the most affectionate memories I have of Geoff is that he was an inveterate potterer. Of course he would also have periods of feverish activity, preparing for his television programmes, spending long days shooting, and struggling to meet tight deadlines for his books and newspaper and magazine articles; but his relaxation was to potter about his garden, like Ratty on the river bank. He would do this endlessly – a lick of paint here, a bit of tying in there and frequent spells of gentle hoeing in his vegetable garden.

But the place where he liked to potter most was the greenhouse. He was bitten by the bug when he was about ten years old and our dad saw an advertisement in the local paper for an old, second-hand wooden greenhouse. We had to dismantle it ourselves and get it home, which was a problem because it would not fit into the Ford Popular our dad had at the time. So we borrowed the boy scouts' 'trek-cart' (as it was romantically known), a rickety wooden construction with iron-bound wheels. This we trundled up the main A10 road (no traffic in those days), about one and a half miles to the owner's house. He led us into his back garden and there it stood – practically no glass, some rotting timbers and a distinctly leaning look about it. But it was a greenhouse and they were hard to come by, so we bought it. I think Dad paid about £2 for it, which was a lot to him in those days.

After dismantling it, itself no easy task, we faced the awful prospect of trundling the now loaded trek-cart back home up the A10. Eventually, hot and tired and looking like Steptoe and Two Sons, we got it home and erected it. Dad had been a carpenter in the RAF during the Second World War, so he set to repairing it. Then he bought some second-hand timber from the demolition yard (we both offered a prayer that it would fit into the Ford Popular, and it did – good old God!) and made some staging.

An old lady called Matty Spicer, who lived in a huge, rambling house near by, heard about our adventures and offered us a gigantic pile of terracotta pots of all shapes and sizes, and hundreds of wooden seed trays – for nothing. So the old and by now complaining Ford Popular was again pressed into service and, after a weekend of to-ing and fro-ing, we ended up with a pile of pots and boxes that dwarfed the greenhouse. We had more than they had at Kew gardens!

This was the defining moment in Geoff's career. It was what gave the

Opposite: Annuals, grown in containers filled with coir, can be started in the greenhouse and will provide a brilliant display throughout the year.

Above: Dad in one of his more serious moods in the greenhouse at our house in Broxbourne.

Above right: Geoff aged about sixteen with his beloved chrysanthemums.

Right: The family on a day out in our old faithful Ford Popular. (Note the Homburg hat and the school blazers.)

first impetus to a long adventure that lasted for the rest of his life. It was not getting his first commission to write for *Garden News*, his first venture into television or even his first sight of Barnsdale that did this. It was Matty Spicer, an old, slightly batty but very kind old lady giving him some pots. What that generous act did was start a kind of partnership between Geoff and our father, himself a kind and slightly batty man, in establishing a greenhouse venture that would eventually rival the best.

I was appointed vegetable supremo and Geoff and Dad were grandees of the greenhouse, with joint responsibilities for the ornamental garden. I gave them orders for the vegetable plants that I wanted to be started in the greenhouse, and they also grew tomatoes, cucumbers and a whole range of ornamental plants. Their favourites were chrysanthemums and carnations.

He grew giant blooms, which he preened and protected as though they were his children. When he stood them outside the greenhouse he erected an elaborate structure for them, and covered them with a great, green, army-surplus tarpaulin to protect them from the rain (polythene had not yet been invented). He would even, occasionally, get up in the night to comfort them and reassure them that they were safe. I suspect a little battiness had been passed down in the paternal genes.

THE FIRST GLASSHOUSE JOB

From the greenhouse it was a short step to his first, pre-college job in a tomato nursery in the Lea Valley. He worked for Jack Alison, a good man who cared about his young workers and was keen to pass on his considerable knowledge and experience. So by the time Geoff left Jack a year later he knew a great deal about the commercial growing of tomatoes. But when he reflected on this he realized that he had spent the whole year pinching out laterals, tying in, feeding and watering. Not an exciting way to spend one's life, he thought. He determined that when he was at college studying horticulture he would begin to develop the more creative aspects of his work. It was this determination which led him to establish a landscaping business after he left college and ultimately into journalism.

But all the time he kept close to his greenhouse, extending it and expanding into his first polythene tunnel to supply plants for his landscaping work. He continued with these up to the time he moved into Barnsdale, when he began to realize his dream of creating a complex of glasshouses in which he could grow the whole range of plants that interested him. His first priority clearly had to be a propagating house, so that he could raise the thousands of plants he would need to stock Barnsdale and where he could show his viewers how it was done. Choosing the right structure for the job was important, as it is to every gardener.

CHOOSING A GREENHOUSE

Greenhouses come in all shapes, sizes and materials, all with advantages and disadvantages, so you should take good care to pick the one that suits your own conditions and your pocket. For the gardener there is little point in trying to do the things a commercial grower would do. There are really only four aspects you will need to consider: cost, space, aesthetics and maintenance.

When considering what size of greenhouse to buy remember that it is most gardeners' experience that as their enthusiasm flourishes and grows so their greenhouse seems to get smaller and smaller. So the general rule should be: get the biggest structure you can afford, as long as you have the space. You will never regret it.

Then you will have to wrestle with the balance between aesthetics and cost. Wooden greenhouses look very good, but they are expensive and need regular maintenance. Aluminium is cheaper and needs no maintenance; and in fact there are some attractive models now on the market, which may solve the aesthetics problem as well. For the enthusiast with a small garden a hexagonal greenhouse may be the answer. They can be bought in aluminium or wood and make maximum use of space by reducing the standing and working area.

Plastic structures are by no means the prettiest of greenhouses, but if that is not an issue they are worth considering because they are by far the cheapest. Kits to build them can be bought from good garden centres. The plastic sheet will have to be replaced every three or four years, but apart from that they need no maintenance. Take care to keep them as clean as you can because they are not as good as glass as conductors of light.

GREENHOUSE MANAGEMENT

Staging All greenhouse manufacturers will supply staging but if this is an expense too far you can always make your own. I was lucky, because Geoff showed me how to make mine. It was made with a view to removing it each season, after the early plants had been put outside to harden off, to make room for the tomatoes, cucumbers, aubergines, peppers and melons that I grow in the summer. (Actually my wife grows the plants, but I did make the staging.) I simply made a slatted shelf out of 5cm x 2.5cm (2in x 1in) timber, fitted with 5cm x 5cm (2in x 2in) wooden legs attached by coach bolts. The back of the shelf is attached to the side of the greenhouse, so that it makes a good, solid structure. I covered the slats with a piece of marine plywood, cut to size, which I covered in turn with a piece of heavy-gauge polythene. Finally I covered this with a sheet of capillary matting (see page 65). I was delighted when Geoff showed me the capillary matting dodge – it solves all watering problems. Just flood the matting and the plants are watered – particularly good if you are growing in coir.

Heating Small electric space heaters are very convenient and can be cheap to run, provided you get one fitted with a thermostat. If you have no electricity supply to your greenhouse Geoff always recommended a bottled gas heater. Paraffin heaters are available, but they are inconvenient and tend to produce unhealthy fumes which could damage young seedlings unless you are fastidious about keeping the wick trimmed.

If you are worried about the cost of heating you can insulate the

Even a small greenhouse will bestow endless pleasure in the form of colourful flowers and copious supplies of vegetable plants.

greenhouse in winter by fitting panels of polystyrene below the staging and bubble polythene to the glazing bars above. These would, of course, have to be removed when the temperature rises in spring.

A maximum and minimum thermometer is essential for the control of heat because it allows you to check that the temperature has not dropped too far or risen too high during the night, thus helping you to get maximum heat efficiency for your money.

An aluminium greenhouse can be an inexpensive way to expand your gardening activity enormously – and will pay for itself in no time.

Ventilation You must ensure good ventilation as lack of air circulation encourages fungus diseases, even in the winter. If you use gas or paraffin heaters you should always have at least one light open a crack, to let out any noxious fumes. In the summer, of course, you will need a vigorous circulation of air to keep diseases at bay and to keep the temperature down. Some good automatic ventilators are available now which automatically open and close the lights as the temperature rises and falls – very useful for the gardener who spends all day at work and does not want to have to guess each morning what the weather is going to do.

Above left: Geoff chose the cheap way to shade his greenhouse, with a paint-on shading, which he took care to remove when the sun's strength began to wane.

Above right: Damping down is an important job, especially on hot days.

Shading In the summer, in the unlikely event of some hot sunshine, you will probably need to shade your greenhouse to protect the plants from sunburn. Sun cream is not a satisfactory solution! Blinds are available, for fitting to either the inside or the outside of the glass, but they are fairly expensive. The cheaper alternative is to buy a can of shading paint, which will protect during the summer and can be washed off during the winter.

Propagating with bottom heat For propagation you will obtain the best results if you provide some bottom heat. If you have only a few plants an electric propagator is sufficient, but Geoff taught me a far better method using a heated blanket, which can be bought from a garden centre or nursery supplier. I put a piece of 2.5cm (1in) polystyrene on to the plywood base of my staging and lay the blanket on top. I then cover the whole thing with strong polythene to protect it from water, put capillary matting on the top, and I have a large heated bench. I set the thermostat to about 18°C (65°F) and if anything needs more heat I put it under a polythene cloche; if it needs less I stand it on a upturned seed tray. Geoff earns a word of thanks every year.

Watering It is best to water seedlings with water that is at the same temperature as the greenhouse. To do this you will need a tank in the greenhouse that you fill every day, before you knock off. If you only have room to store the tank under the staging Geoff had another staggeringly simple idea: simply stand the tank on three broomstick rollers, so that you can easily pull it out to fill the can. An even easier way for the smaller greenhouse is to buy yourself a couple of watering cans and keep them in the greenhouse at night.

Seedlings are best watered with a can, fitted with a fine rose. It is worth spending a bit of money on a good watering can with a long spout, so that you can reach the back of the staging – and the ones with the holes in the top of the rose are particularly good. Dear old Geoff bought me a beauty for Christmas, the year before he died. I think about him every time I use it.

Never flood seeds or you will wash them all to one side of the tray. If you use capillary matting, however, you will never need to water from above – just keep the matting wet, except in winter. If you use this method the compost in the seed tray should be well watered before the seeds are sown in it. After sowing, cover the seeds with vermiculite, if they are to be grown on indoors, or fine horticultural grit if they are to be grown on in a cold frame. Then you can simply water the capillary matting for those grown inside. Overhead watering is safe for those grown in the cold frame.

In the summer when the young plants are bigger, you can water them with a hose, which will be much quicker than using a can. There are also a number of quite sophisticated lances, wands, jets and spray attachments on the market, so you should shop around to see what suits you best.

You will also need to 'damp down' the greenhouse in the summer, by spraying the paths and the soil under the staging to provide a good, humid atmosphere. Misting systems and trickle irrigation are available, but pretty costly.

Seed and potting composts If you use a peat-based compost, you can of course expect Geoff to be frowning at you from above and he could even launch the odd thunderbolt. There are many different brands of organic compost on the market and you should use a little trial and error to see which one suits you best. I have used a standard brand of coir compost for about seven years and have never had a failure I can attribute to compost. There are two grades, one for seeds and one for potting, both of which come with a slow-release fertilizer, which means they won't need feeding for about two months. You will go a long way to beat it.

For plants that are to be grown in containers outside many gardeners prefer to use a soil-based compost such as John Innes; but John Innes composts contain peat, which is not a good option for anyone wishing to follow Geoff's principles. Home-made soil-based compost is usually a mixture of loam (which is produced from rotting stacked turf), sand and peat,

Sowing lettuce in a tray of coir compost.

with some added nutrients, but coir can be substituted for peat. Traditionally the ratio is of about 7 parts loam, 3 parts coir and 2 parts sharp sand, with a little blood, fish and bone manure added. Geoff mixed his own compost, using much the same recipe as that for John Innes compost but substituting coir for peat, and he preferred this for containers that were to stand outside because it is more water retentive. It is also a heavier medium and this prevents the container from blowing over in a high wind.

GROWING IN COLD FRAMES

Types of frame If you have a greenhouse you will almost certainly want a cold frame as well, for gradually acclimatizing plants to the colder conditions they will meet outside. A frame is also useful for growing tender plants later in the year, when your greenhouse is full of tomatoes and other goodies. Geoff seemed to be forever knocking up a frame for some new garden he was building. Almost all garden centres and greenhouse manufacturers sell frames, in either wood or aluminium. These come in a variety of types, including frames that you can fix to the wall of the house or shed. Make sure you choose the size carefully, erring on the large side, if you have the space and the money. A lot of people make their own frames (see page 81). If, however, you are not a handy carpenter, the alternative is to buy a sheet of rigid horticultural plastic and fix it to a simple wooden frame that can be rested on the top. At a pinch, I have often used a large plastic cloche as a cold frame, with perfectly satisfactory results. In fact, Geoff showed that if you are growing only a small number of plants there is nothing wrong with an orange box,

Below left: A simple home-made cold frame is useful for hardening off and for protecting plants from cold and wet.

Below right: Ventilation must be gradually increased to acclimatise plants to lower temperatures.

insulated with some polystyrene, with a sheet of glass or plastic on the top and a couple of string handles on the sides. He used to trot it out every year on *Gardeners' World*. They called it the 'carrycot frame'.

HARDENING OFF

Frames are invaluable for hardening off – that is, gradually acclimatizing plants grown indoors to the lower temperatures outside. When you have a batch of plants that are ready, or almost ready, for planting outside, put them out into the cold frame and gradually increase the amount of air they are given by day, so that they do not go into a state of shock. When the frame is open all day, start opening it a fraction at night and increase the amount until it is wide open all night as well. However, keep a close eye on the weather forecast and close down completely if there is any threat of frost. If there is likely to be a really hard frost a couple of old sacks draped over the top of the frame will ensure complete protection.

SOWING IN FRAMES

Cold frames are also useful for sowing spring and summer seeds of hardy annuals, herbaceous perennials and most hardy vegetables. Many of these need no heat for germination, but will be grateful for the protection from wind and cold rain afforded by the frame.

In winter, the cold frame can be used for the germination of seeds such as alpines and other plants that require low temperatures for germination. The covering of the frame will not protect the emerging plants entirely from freezing temperatures, but this will do no harm. They will be protected from excessive rain, which will help growth. They should be ventilated a little day and night, even in the coldest temperatures.

OTHER USES FOR THE FRAME

Cold frames can also be used like a cloche, by cultivating the base and growing early and late crops directly in the soil.

If the base is lined with a layer of wet sand the frame can be valuable for rooting cuttings, which will appreciate the humid atmosphere this creates. You can either put them into pots or trays and stand them directly on the sand, or you can put a layer of compost on to the sand and root them into that. In either case the cuttings should be covered with a sheet of thin polythene to conserve moisture.

MAKING A COLD FRAME

For the top of the cold frame you can use wooden glazing bars and glass; alternatively you can use a sheet of rigid horticultural plastic and fix it to a simple wooden frame of whatever size you can fit into your garden.

For the base of the cold frame, use pressure-treated or recycled timber – Geoff suggested old floorboards – treated with preservative and paint the frame with a waterproof paint. A sloping top for the lid allows the plants inside to receive maximum light and rain to drain off. Handles enable you to position the frame on bare soil where you want it.

CLOCHES

Cloches are used to extend the growing season at both ends and can give you as much as 4–6 weeks of extra growing time. They provide a warmer climate, protected from rain and wind, to promote growth.

Rigid plastic cloches are available commercially, but tend to be expensive. Single-row cloches can be made easily, using wire hoops with a sheet of polythene stretched over the top. The polythene should be anchored at either end by burying it in the soil.

Larger cloches can be bought, for the protection of deep beds or larger areas of crops. These are made from heavy gauge polythene stretched over metal frames. They are efficient and convenient, but pretty pricey, and in my experience the covers last only three or four years, after which you will have to replace them, which will stretch the pocket further.

Geoff taught me how to avoid this expense with his ingenious tunnel cloche. The most important thing to do when using cloches for early crops is to remember to put them into place two or three weeks before sowing or planting crops. This will allow the soil to warm up well in advance, providing an inviting environment for your plants or seeds.

GROWING UNDER FLAT PLASTIC

Early crops can also be grown successfully just by laying polythene on the soil, burying the edges to keep it from floating away and planting through

MAKING A TUNNEL CLOCHE

Cut some 20mm (3/4in) alkathene water pipe into 1.8m (6ft) lengths to form hoops and push a piece of dowel into each end. Drill a small hole through the pipe

and the dowel and push a nail through the hole to secure it. Push the dowels into the soil about 1.25m (4ft) apart and cover them with polythene.

Bury the polythene at each end of the row of hoops to secure it. Tighten the polythene with string tied from the nail at the bottom of each hoop, passed over

the top and secured to the nail on the other side, to keep the wind from getting under it.

Access to the beds for ventilation during warm weather is obtained simply by lifting the polythene sheet.

holes cut in the plastic. I use black plastic because by keeping out the light it keeps the weeds down.

I have found this method particularly effective for growing very early potatoes, which I plant in early February and I am usually eating potatoes by mid-May or very early June. The thing to remember is to protect them from frost by covering them with horticultural fleece, straw, old newspapers or any other insulating material. If you use fleece you will only protect them from one or two degrees of frost, but don't worry – the crop will easily recover, although you may harvest later.

Strawberries growing under a black plastic sheet to mulch them and suppress weeds.

GROWING TECHNIQUES

Sowing seeds As I have said earlier, seeds should be grown in a seed compost, and the best and most environmentally friendly is probably coir seed compost. Fill the pot, tray or module with compost and tap it down to just below the top of the container. Cut yourself a piece of wood the same size and shape as the container, to use as a presser for gently consolidating the compost. You should then have a nice flat surface on which to sow the seed. Water well before sowing, using a fine rose. Sow the seeds thinly and cover with vermiculite if they are small or need light to germinate. You will find this information on the seed packet. If they are large they can be covered with compost. For seeds that will be

Geoff was never happier than when he was working in his greenhouse, as this picture of him with a lovely display of cinerarias demonstrates.

grown with no heat in the cold frame, cover with a layer of fine horticultural grit, which will inhibit weeds and discourage birds from taking the seed when the frame is open. If you are growing seeds to become single plants in pots or modules it is a good idea to sow two, for insurance purposes: if only one germinates you are OK and if two germinate you simply pull one out. Put the containers on to a heated bench or propagator if possible, ensuring that you choose the correct heat conditions for each variety. If they are on a bench it is wise to cover them with thin, clear polythene, so as to conserve as much moisture as possible. Note that there are a few seeds that require dark conditions for germination, so be sure to read the packet carefully and use opaque polythene if germination in the dark is called for.

You should inspect newly sown seeds daily and, as soon as the first signs of germination appear remove the polythene and give the emerging seedlings as much light as possible, although strong, hot sunlight should be avoided, especially if the leaves are wet. In this case shelter the plants with sheets of newspaper while the sun is on them, but don't forget to remove it as soon as possible as the exclusion of light will make the plants long and spindly. My wife, Carol, used to work for Geoff in his greenhouses and on Friday nights she would always remind him to look at the covered seedlings to see if they had germinated. He would always forget and Carol would return on Monday to find stalky seedlings falling all over the staging like spaghetti in an Italian restaurant. 'Well,' he would say, 'nobody's perfect.'

When the plants are large enough to handle you should transfer them to a larger container, using fresh compost and spacings of about 3–4 cm (1–1½ in), depending on the size of the plant. Ease the seedling out of the compost with a stick, always handling it by the leaves to avoid damage to the plant, and transfer it to a planting hole in the new compost, ensuring that the roots go right to the bottom of the hole, so that the leaves are at compost level. Finally, gently firm the compost at one side of the plant, to ensure that it is in contact with the roots.

If the seedlings are too small to handle (as may be the case with plants such as lobelia and begonias), prick them out in small clumps and they will grow on happily as single plants. Water well when the container is full and place it in full light. If you are not using capillary matting you will have to water every day, but remember not to overdo it.

Cuttings Are a cheap and satisfying way to increase your stock of plants or to replace those that are getting old and losing their vigour. It is also sensible to take cuttings of tender plants which you could lose in the event of hard frosts. Not all cuttings require a greenhouse for growing on, but it is a necessity for most plants. Here are some of the most common methods.

TAKING BASAL CUTTINGS

Cut off the shoot with a sharp knife, as close to the base of the plant as possible.

Put the shoot into a pot of moist compost and cover the whole thing with a polythene bag. Place the

pot in a warm place in the greenhouse and it will be rooted in no time.

TAKING STEM CUTTINGS

Look for a strong, non-flowering shoot and cut it just below a leaf joint, about 10cm (4in) from the tip.

Take off the lower leaves and dip the shoot into hormone rooting powder.

Water well and cover with thin polythene. In this case the container can be put into a cold frame, or a cool greenhouse.

Herbaceous perennial cuttings There are two main ways of propagating perennials from cuttings: basal cuttings and stem cuttings, which are taken later in the year:

Basal cuttings Basal cuttings are taken mainly from herbaceous perennials, in spring, from the new shoots that arise right at the base of the plant. Suitable plants include achillea, anaphalis, anthemis, campanula, chrysanthemum, delphinium, dicentra, gypsophila, hesperis, lupins, lychnis, malva and polygonum. There is a variation from this method, called an Irishman's cutting. This entails taking a small amount of root with the cutting, thus getting the best of both worlds.

Stem cuttings Stem cuttings are usually taken from June onwards. Suitable plants include acaena, ajuga, artemisia, ballota, centaurea, dianthus, diascia, euphorbia, gypsophila, helenium, helichrysum, lysimachia, penstemon, phlomis, sedum and teudrium. Tender perennials, such as fuchsias, argyranthemums and geraniums, can be treated in this way too, to provide a good supply of plants for the following year. Perennials with tuberous roots, however, such as dahlias, perennial salvias and cosmos, are treated differently. As soon as the tops have been touched by the first frost they should be cut down to about 7cm (3in), lifted and allowed to dry for a few hours. Store the roots in a box packed round with compost or soil, and keep them, almost completely dry, in a cool, frost-free place. In spring

TAKING SOFTWOOD CUTTINGS

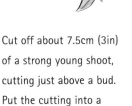

Cut off about 7.5cm (3in) of a strong young shoot, cutting just above a bud. Put the cutting into a polythene bag immediately.

Remove the lower leaves with a sharp knife and dip the cutting into a copper fungicide for safe measure.

Dibble the cutting into a pot of coir compost, putting about four cuttings into each 10cm (4in) pot. Cover the pot with thin polythene to preserve humidity.

bring them into full light and begin to water them, and strong young shoots will begin to grow. Detach these when they are about 8cm (3 ¹/₂in) long and trim them in the usual way, by cutting just below a leaf joint. Trim off the lower leaves, dip the cuttings into copper fungicide and then into hormone rooting powder, and put them into a pot or box of compost. A little bottom heat is ideal for them and if you can cover them with a small plastic cloche on the bench, this will preserve the humid atmosphere they need.

When they have rooted they can be potted on and finally put into a cold frame to slowly acclimatize to lower temperatures.

Softwood cuttings of shrubs Softwood cuttings are perhaps the best and easiest way to propagate shrubs. Geoff was ceaselessly taking softwood cuttings, with great success. These cuttings are best taken in late spring or early summer, although you should not be put off taking them if you are a little late. As long as some soft growth is available you should be OK following the instructions given above.

When you cover the pot with thin polythene, to preserve humidity, make sure the polythene just touches the leaves, to avoid condensation, and tuck it under the pot to get a hermetic seal. Finally put the pot into a shaded cold frame, so that it is out of direct sunlight.

Softwood cuttings can take from three weeks to about six months to root. Just leave them alone until you see some signs of life.

The wonga-wonga vine
Pandorea pandorana
'Golden Shower'.

CONSERVATORIES FOR THE GREENHOUSE EFFECT

Geoff had always coveted his neighbour's conservatory. He wanted somewhere to relax when it was cold or raining and he couldn't indulge in contemplation time in the garden. He wanted to be surrounded by exotic plants and share a glass or two of wine with Lynda there, but he was going to have to wait until he had been at Barnsdale for twelve years before he could afford it. He was a man who was prepared to wait until he could do it properly because he had very strong feelings about the need to build something that blends sensitively with the house and garden. He had seen enough of grotesque plastic structures growing like tumours on gentle old houses that were clearly feeling uncomfortable.

For days he and Lynda would walk around Barnsdale, looking for a suitable wall to hang the conservatory on – and he began to feel more and more uncomfortable: Barnsdale was begging him not to do it. He wanted a conservatory, but in the end, Barnsdale won. Geoff decided that he would build a detached conservatory just beyond the wall of the small courtyard that his back door opened on to. This experience led him to the firm view that the first rule of getting a conservatory was to choose it carefully, ensuring that it fitted with your house and garden.

If you want to grow plants in the conservatory make sure it is suitable for this purpose. For example, the plantsman or woman will want some staging, which means that you will need a way of disposing of the water that is bound to be splashed about. This will mean a tiled or paved floor, rather than fitted carpet. The staging should have a 10cm (4in) lip all round so that it can be filled with sand, which will keep the plants moist and provide the humidity they so urgently need.

It will also need particularly good ventilation, because conservatories have a tendency to get very, very hot. In Geoff's conservatory he had roof lights which ran end to end, both sides of the ridge, as well as extra vents in the side and in the bottom brick wall, too. He had blinds fitted, so that they could be drawn on the hottest days for shading. And don't forget that heating will be required for cold weather, in just the same way as for the greenhouse.

Beds can be made in the conservatory and these have the great advantage that they will keep the roots of the plants cool. Geoff started by planting climbers in the narrow beds he had built and also in pots. If you're planting pots, go for clay ones as plastic tends to get very hot. For a taste of the exotic you cannot beat bougainvillea, which has masses of red, pink or white flowers and thrives in cool conditions. Geoff liked the wonga-wonga vine *Pandorea pandorana* (well, he would, wouldn't he?), and *Cestrum elegans*, a large shrub with clusters of huge red flowers. There are also smaller plants

such as lachenalias which have long tubular flowers of red, orange or pale blue, or nemesias which seem to flower for ever. If you go to a specialist nursery or a really good garden centre you will find plenty of wonderful plants to choose from. Geoff, in one of his articles, said, 'I promise you, you won't want to stop collecting fabulous plants until your new conservatory is packed to the gunwales.' His own conservatory was a testament to this. You needed a machete to get through the door!

Geoff's conservatory was a magnificent confusion of colour and perfume.

89

A touch of old England

GEOFF'S INSPIRATION

When the Second World War began in 1939, Geoff and I were only three years old so, whilst we were aware of extraordinary happenings around us, we had no conception of the disaster in which we had all become involved. But our father had, and he was very conscious of the difficulties he would face in trying to keep his family properly fed and watered.

Shortly after the war began the government introduced its 'Dig For Victory' campaign, exhorting people with dramatic appeals to their patriotism to turn every piece of spare land they had over to food production. Our father, ever proud to be British, set to work with his spade and, much to our mother's distress, dug up the flower garden and the lawns, dismantled our little rose arbour, took away any unnecessary ornamentation and turned the garden all over to vegetables. The only exception to his 'scorched earth' policy was a chicken house, which he built himself from old timber we had in the garden – he even sacrificed parts of the fence when the timber supply ran out. Nothing stood in the way of this grimly determined man who was firmly set on a course of survival.

Our garden remained like this for the whole course of the war and a little time after. As Geoff and I grew older, we were roped in to help with the weeding, sowing and planting – and thus were sown, too, the seeds of a lifelong passion in both of us. But what none of us realized at the time was that our father, with his defiant urge to win the battle, had, in fact, created a medieval-style cottage garden. In medieval times cottage dwellers had no other way to feed themselves, so they set out to use their garden to make themselves self-sufficient, in just the same way that our father had done. The better-off cottagers would also have a pig, and maybe a few chickens, ducks or geese.

Dad never got a pig. It was often mooted, while we sat round the kitchen table eating our largely vegetarian meals, but Mother was adamant – quite unreasonably, we thought – that no pig would cross our threshold, with its uncivilized smells and gruntings. Well, we lived in a middle-class residential area, so perhaps she had a point.

I believe that it was this experience that led to Geoff's love of the cottage garden style. It inspired in him a deep-down feeling that the garden, as well as being beautiful, should be useful. He loved his borders and he was a great plantsman, but he was never happier than when he was hoeing through his onions or wheeling a barrowload of potatoes into store.

Opposite: The Artisan's Garden, randomly planted in cottage garden style, and with its love seat for contemplation and repose, brings a touch of nostalgia for the tranquillity of the old country gardens.

Opposite: Camp Cottage, one of the delightful locations Geoff used for the *Gardeners' World* 'Cottage Gardens' series.

THE GERM OF AN IDEA

Geoff always had a great affinity with the people who worked allotments (more of which on page 143). The thing that fascinated him most about these small parcels of land, often surrounded by smoking factory chimneys or crowded housing estates, was the wonderland of old sheds, improvised greenhouses, rusty baths, gargantuan structures for the support of runner beans and a whole variety of inventive ways to make something out of nothing. Most allotments are an Aladdin's cave of treasures, all made to make the garden useful. Many allotmenteers would grow flowers for cutting as well as vegetables, so that they could carry home a bounteous cargo to feed the family as well as bring a breath of the outside into the house. These allotment holders were the modern equivalent to the cottage gardener of old.

An idea began to germinate in Geoff's mind. It occurred to him that the English cottage garden with its simplicity and unpretentious nature would make the ideal vehicle for showing his viewers how to combine peace and beauty with fruitful ways to help to support the family. He decided that he would try to persuade the BBC to make a series of six programmes about cottage gardens. Well, he did not have to try very hard: the idea was taken up enthusiastically and he was on his way.

He felt strongly that in order to have a cottage garden you do not have to have a cottage. Certainly, in his television series, Geoff showed some idyllic cottages, tucked away in the heart of the country and surrounded by stunningly beautiful gardens. But he also showed modern houses, sometimes on large estates, which had equally lovely gardens in the cottage garden style and which brought a great sense of tranquillity into a rather more harsh environment.

His original idea was to make a series centred around the gardens of working-class men and women, because that was where it all began, and is what the true cottage garden is all about. His theme would be based on the Victorian cottage garden, because although the Victorians didn't originate the idea of 'useful and beautiful' gardens they developed it, for during the Industrial Revolution and the days of the Empire more people had a little more time for beauty and no longer needed to focus just on survival. What he wanted was a series about gardens cared for by hard-bitten men who came home from t'mill in braces and shirts with no collars and tended big leeks, or indomitable ladies who would cycle home, with baskets on the handlebars, from teaching at the local school, to get out into their gardens and do the same. He was a bit resistant to the idea of 'chocolate-box' cottages set in the stockbroker belts around London, with pretty gardens lovingly tended by a team of professional gardeners. But then he thought

Self-seeding plants, which most of the plants in this border are, provide the cheapest and most beautiful way to enhance your borders.

that in today's affluent society there was a demand for ideas and information from people who had a bob or two to spend on their gardens but still wanted to maintain a cottage garden atmosphere. So he decided to cover both styles, and create two cottage gardens.

The first he called the Artisan's Garden, which was to be about the use of cheap materials and improvization, while the second was called the Gentleman's Garden, still based on cottage garden principles, but on which more money would be spent, although he accepted that it would not necessarily be within the budget of all his viewers and readers. Both parts of the programme would be run alongside each other, to maintain interest and to enable the ideas from one to cross-pollinate with the other. The basic thinking behind the design of the two gardens was that ideas from both could be incorporated into viewers' and readers' own gardens. After all, these days most people start as 'artisans' and slowly graduate to becoming 'gentlemen'.

The programme was made for the BBC by Catalyst Television, and Geoff was fortunate enough to be given an inspirational producer called Andrew Gosling who coaxed out of him some wonderfully creative ideas. They decided that the programme would be made over a period of two years, which enabled them to introduce some stunning effects, by showing each garden being built in Geoff's helpful step-by-step style and then, immediately afterwards, showing what the garden would look like in a year's time. The result was electric! I always felt motivated to get up out of my chair at nine o'clock in the evening and start building straight away.

The Artisan's Garden

The design for the Artisan's Garden was essentially simple and straightforward. The whole point about any cottage garden is that it is designed first for utility, not for some airy-fairy artistic concept. And it is constantly changing: it will evolve as your ideas evolve and you realize your mistakes. Geoff's original design could not have been simpler: just four central beds connected by a path and the whole thing surrounded by a further bed around the perimeter. Geoff was not only a brilliant designer, but the ideas he put into his writing and his television were always based on the premise that whatever he described had to be carried out by people who were not necessarily skilled designers, plantspeople, bricklayers, paviours or carpenters. They had to be essentially practical, down to earth and within the reach of both the skills and the pockets of his viewers or readers.

It was this view, coupled with the fact that any true artisan would be inclined to keep the garden simple and practical, that led him to design it in modules, connected by paths. These could easily be arranged to suit the shape of the garden plot and the position of the house so that they could be managed easily by a man or woman who had little time and possibly little energy after a hard day's work.

HEDGING AGAINST INVASION

Geoff decided to enclose the Artisan's Garden with a combination of hedging and fencing.

For the hedge he chose his favourite hedge plant for a cottage garden, the traditional hawthorn, which can be clipped into an excellent, dense screen to look superb all year – planted about 30cm (12in) apart as described on pages 18–19. If you have the space to be more informal you can grow honeysuckle and eglantine or dog roses through it, which will not only make it look like the edge of paradise but will also attract birds and insects. The birds will give you a chorus of music and both will feed gratefully on the pests which may also visit your garden. Geoff persuaded me to plant dog roses in my own garden hedge and they look magnificent. They have been supplemented by a delightful woodbine, or wild honeysuckle, which must have self-seeded; with no announcement or introduction, it just appeared to take its place in the tapestry of the hedge. Berberis, beech, hornbeam or holly are some of the many other plants that will also make a useful hedge.

Owl Cottage, another of Geoff's locations, where hedges are used inventively to give glimpses of the lovely thatched cottage.

1 Planted container

2 Bench

3 Herb table

4 Tool chest

5 Cold frame

6 Compost bin

7 Vegetables in deep beds

8 Herb planting

9 Clipped box (*Buxus sempervirens*)

10 Mixed planting of shrubs and herbaceous perennials throughout garden

11 Obelisk

12 Arbour

13 Gravel path

14 Picket fence

15 Arch

Opposite: The confusion of colour and light in the Artisan's Garden supplies a never-ending delight and a sense of peace.

Left: The Iceland poppy grows in profusion in the Artisan's Garden.

Right: Ferns are wonderful foliage plants and thrive in shady, damp conditions.

Ramming in the posts
for the picket fence,
whilst checking the
level.

FENCING AS A FOIL

As Geoff was a romantic, his favourite form of fencing for the cottage garden was the picket fence, which would have featured in most Victorian country cottages. There was also a practical reason for his preference. Not only is picket fencing more attractive than other kinds of fencing, but it lets in more sunlight to the garden, providing plants with the warmth and the light they need.

Panel fencing tends to present an impenetrable barrier, shutting off views of the surrounding countryside; but on the other hand it is cheap, easy to erect and the dreadful orange colour it is normally supplied in can be overcome by painting it with dark green matt paint, to make it look more hedge-like. Geoff used a mixture of both types of fencing in his Artisan's Garden: a picket fence at the front and panel fencing, painted dark green, at the sides. This was partly because he felt that most people would wish to preserve some privacy and also because the television programme had to be made without distraction from outside the garden.

The main things to observe when erecting a fence are:

1 Make sure the fence is straight, by using a line to mark out its position, and make sure your posts are upright, by using a spirit level.

2 If you concrete the posts into the ground they will quickly rot off at the base unless they are pressure-treated. If you use the type of metal socket which is driven into the ground your fence is likely to be unstable, particularly in stony ground. It is better to use the type of socket designed to be concreted into the ground, so that the post is not in contact with the concrete.

3 For panel fencing, don't put all the posts in first and try to fit the panels to them. You are sure to get your measurements wrong and you only need to be a centimetre out for you to have a disaster. Erect the fence as shown in the diagram opposite, repeating the process until the fence is completed. (Geoff taught me the simple dodge of doing it this way after collapsing with laughter when he caught me in the act of trying to put up panel fencing. He could be a very irritating man at times.)

4 Paling fencing can be bought in 1.8m (6ft) panels but it can easily be made yourself if you have any skills with the saw and hammer. In this case, put the posts in first, having measured carefully, and nail 7.5 x 2.5cm (3 x 1in) horizontal bars to the posts after you have allowed the concrete to set for about three days. Then you can nail the palings, which are made from

7.5 x 2cm (3 x $^3/_4$in) timber, to the horizontals and the job's done.

5 Geoff, who was not a great respecter of civic dignity, suggested that, if you have the space, you should pinch a tiny bed in front of your paling fence and the authorities will rarely object as the result is usually so attractive. I think we should all rise up in support of Geoff on this, and if the council objects we should build barricades in the streets.

GATES AND ARCHES

To the picket fence at the front of his Artisan's Garden Geoff added what the cottagers of old would have used: a wicket gate. These can be bought ready made, or, if you are handy in the workshop, you can make your own. Alternatively, if you have used a different kind of fencing or a hedge – or, if you are really lucky, you may have a wall – you may want to use one of the many other designs of gate that are available. The only thing that Geoff felt really strongly about was the use of wrought iron, which, whilst fine elsewhere, he thought would be completely out of place in the cottage garden.

He also added a wooden arch over the gate to the Artisan's Garden, as

ERECTING A PANEL FENCE

Put the first post in and offer the first panel up to it, supporting it at the right height with bricks or wooden blocks.

Nail the panel to the first post and then offer the second post up to the first panel and concrete it in. Repeat the process until the fence is completed.

a further authentic touch. With the arch the Victorians, ever conscious of their own mortality, were probably imitating the church lychgate, which provided a place to rest the coffin until the parson was ready, but the cottage dwellers made it a thing of beauty. Geoff loved arches because they add height to the garden and you can grow beautiful climbers up them, such as honeysuckle or roses, giving you a perfumed entrance each time you come through.

A bird's-eye view of the Artisan's Garden, showing the arched gate and an abundance of flowers behind.

PATHS FOR PLEASURE AND PURPOSE
Having got the garden properly enclosed, Geoff's next job was to lay the paths. His view was that this needed to be done cheaply, so no paving of any kind was considered for this garden. No Victorian farm worker could have afforded it and that is also probably true of many a young couple who have just bought a house and have little money left to spend on the garden.

Geoff opted for gravel paths, which are easy to lay and much cheaper than paving. They also make an attractive setting for borders, particularly when plants begin to spill over on to the path. He felt that, although it was not essential to edge the paths, it would make them look neater and he used timber nailed to pegs in the ground for this job. He set the timbers about 7.5cm (3in) above the level of the path to give room to lay bricks or paving at a later date. Setting the timbers at this height also ensures that the beds can be dug, incorporating lots of manure, without the soil spilling all over the path.

There are many other attractive materials that could be used for edging – engineering bricks, for instance, set at forty-five degrees, but these are expensive. If you can get genuine Victorian scalloped or scrolled edging tiles you will have the bee's knees, but you should expect to pay a lot for those too. Imitations can be bought at garden centres – not as nice and still expensive, but attractive.

The gravel will need weeding about twice a year. Take care not to remove the flowering plants that will self-seed in the places that are not frequently trodden. You will also have to top up the gravel from time to time as it will get trodden into the soil, but this problem should get easier as the years go by.

GEOFF'S WOODEN INVENTIONS

Don't ever believe that having an identical set of genes is enough to make twins identical – it isn't! Geoff and I used to have woodwork classes at school and I can well remember my distress at seeing Geoff finish his perfect, beautifully designed butler's tray while I was still struggling with my grossly imperfect little letter rack. He never became a great carpenter, but unlike me he did develop an almost instinctive flair for making wood work for him, and he produced artefacts and ornaments that gave me enormous pleasure (and a hint of envy) and were good enough to show on his broadcasts to the nation.

He wanted to put a number of wooden items into the Artisan's Garden because he knew that wood was all Victorian cottage gardeners would have had to work with – although sometimes they might have been able to barter some skill with the blacksmith for something made from metal.

THE BENCH

Geoff believed that as every gardener needed a rest from time to time, a good solid bench was a must. He made the one for the Artisan's Garden, from pressure-treated softwood which he finished with a blue-grey stain

GEOFF'S WOODEN BENCH AND HERB TABLE

This simple wooden bench can be made easily and cheaply by any but the most ham-fisted gardener, equipped with a saw, a set-square and a screwdriver.

The herb table can be made to whatever size suits your garden. Use substantial timber as it will be subjected to considerable stresses once it is filled with compost.

Measurements for bench:

1 Back: 150 x 38mm (6 x 1½in) timber.

2 Back leg: 50 x 25mm (2 x 1in) timber 75cm (2ft 6in) high.

3 Seat: 150 x 38mm (6 x 1½in) timber x 2.

4 Front leg: 50 x 25mm (2 x 1in) timber 40cm (16in) high.

5 Cross bars: 50 x 25mm (2 x 1in) timber.

Once the herb table is completed and planted with thymes, it will provide a sweet-smelling resting place for your hard-earned cup of tea.

(to the measurements shown on the previous page). You can adjust the length of the bench to fit your own garden.

THE HERB TABLE

This idea was not actually Geoff's; it was one he pinched from his good friend Dan Pearson, the garden designer. He felt it was such a good idea that it had to go into his garden. Fill the box with a mixture of equal parts of soil, coarse grit and compost. The standing-out ground for your cup of tea is made from a few tiles or slates embedded into the top of the compost. Plant it up with thymes, which will soon spread into a living tablecloth that will smell sweet every time you bruise the leaves.

The thing I liked about this was that Geoff got the idea from Dan Pearson. That is exactly the spirit of cottage gardening – an exchange of ideas, plants, produce, seeds and labour. What a lot of problems it would solve if we were all cottage gardeners at heart.

THE ARBOUR

The arbour, or love seat, was Geoff's pride and joy. I first knew he had a penchant for arbours when during our twenty-first birthday party I caught him in the rose arbour in our parents' garden with Skin McCubbin's sister. Ever since I have wondered what he had that I didn't (apart from Skin McCubbin's sister, that is).

In later life Geoff loved to sit and read, or maybe just think, surrounded by the sights, sounds and smells of his lovely garden, preferably with Lynda at his side and perhaps with a good book, a glass of wine and Moss, his dog. This was what he used to call his 'admiring time' – and why not? He felt very strongly that, in the pressured life many of us lead, we should find room for a little quiet admiring time. Although he generally worked like a dog he was a great believer in the restorative powers of a short time spent in the peace and tranquillity of his favourite hidey-hole. You will notice that in almost all the gardens he designed and in all the advice he gave a quiet spot to enjoy all your hard work in the garden was an imperative.

He built his arbour out of planed timber, but other materials could be used: rustic poles, for instance, can be bought cheaply from a garden centre and look good in an older garden. He added a horseshoe that he had dug up out of his garden – and was careful to nail it on with the open side upwards, so that the luck would not run out.

MAKING AN ARBOUR

It is best to make the arbour from planed timber that has been pressure treated. The dimensions can be varied to suit your garden; as a guide, Geoff's was 1.2m (4ft) wide, 75cm (2ft 6in deep) and 2.4m (8ft) high. The corner posts are put into metal sockets that have been concreted into the soil and the final touch is to plant climbing roses and clematis to fill your arbour with perfume.

It is a testament to Geoff's skill and sensitivity that, now that Barnsdale is open to the public, the love seat is never empty. As soon as one couple gets up to move on another couple arrives to take their place. If I know Geoff, he's up there at this very moment arranging romantic interludes for affectionate couples.

THE OBELISK

It was at a stately home — I can't remember which one — that Geoff first got the idea for the obelisk. He could not be said to be delighted by stately homes because he felt uncomfortable being confronted by conspicuous wealth but he had to admit that they often had the most stunning gardens and some wonderful ideas that could be translated into something that the ordinary person could do. The obelisk he saw was made of wrought iron and had probably been designed by somebody with RA after his name. But Geoff, with his scintillating inventiveness, felt that the idea could be carried back and, if he designed it well, made out of wood by anybody with a modicum of carpentry skills.

I went up to Barnsdale to see him the weekend after he had seen it, and was greeted by Geoff, with a childlike grin on his face, saying, 'Come and see my obelisk.' 'Your what?' said I, expecting a grotesque stone structure supporting some kind of statue. He led me down to his embryo Artisan's Garden and showed me a simple, homely structure supporting — what? A

The climbing plants clothing the obelisk that Geoff built in his workshop form a brilliant column of colour and light.

Geoff's brilliant beehive compost bins are easy to construct and make an attractive feature in the garden.

lavatory ballcock float! It was already planted up and looking bare but delightful. Painted in blue-grey, Geoff's obelisk will look good in any cottage garden, planted with sweet peas, clematis or any other climber, although a perfumed one will give most pleasure.

COMPOST BINS

Because the Artisan's Garden was small Geoff did not think the common or garden compost bin (see page 37) would look right – a compost bin had to be more attractive. For this garden and the Gentleman's Garden he had something special up his capacious sleeve. He came up with a design that looks like a beehive. It is built in modules, so that as the compost is removed each part can be taken off, to provide access to the next layer of compost. Again painted blue-grey, it made a very attractive ornament in the garden, it was a brilliant idea. He was so much more inventive than I am that I nearly asked for a DNA test to check our relationship – but one look in the mirror and my doubts were dispelled.

THE COLD FRAME

As Geoff was a great enthusiast for plants grown under glass, in the absence of a greenhouse he was keen to have a cold frame in the Artisan's Garden. He felt it could save lots of money in the purchase of both vegetable and

flowering plants, and therefore would be very useful for a family strapped for cash.

For the sides, brick is far more attractive than wood and, of course, will last a lifetime, as well as retaining heat well in winter, although wood is less expensive and perfectly satisfactory. For the amateur carpenter the difficult part in building a cold frame is the lights for the top, so instead of using wooden glazing bars and glass, Geoff suggested buying window frames. The size of these is dependent, of course, on the size of frame you can fit into your garden and in the design shown on page 81 you may have to vary the dimensions to fit the size of the window frames you buy. Use pressure-treated timber or, if you are worried about the polluting effect this may have, paint the frame with a waterproof paint.

THE TOOL CHEST

This was the most elegant of all Geoff's ideas in the Artisan's Garden. Realizing that he did not have room for a shed, he set out to design a tool chest, so that the tools, watering can, gloves, string and all the other appendages of the cottage gardener could be kept safe and dry. Note especially the crafty support for the sloping lid, so that it can be made level for use as a bench for potting, sowing, taking cuttings and all the other jobs the good gardener needs to do.

This neatly designed tool chest not only provides useful storage space but also doubles as a potting bench when the lid is down. There was also a crafty support for the sloping lid.

An auricula theatre will brighten your fence or wall with a blaze of colour.

THE AURICULA THEATRE

Born about a hundred years too late, Geoff was really a Victorian at heart. His Victorian house was (and still is) filled with a vast collection of Victorian tools, ornaments, paintings and other gubbins. He admired the working-class Victorian, and especially the countryman who spent his time on the farm and in the garden. He could have coped with the privations of the period because with fingers that were green as grass he could have fed his family easily, and he was quite prepared to work exceptionally hard. He would have railed and agitated over Victorian ideas on class, the distribution of wealth, Empire, health care, education, child care, etc., but he would have done just what he did in the twentieth century: put a lot into life and got a lot out, only to give it away the moment he got it.

When Geoff read about the auricula theatres of Victorian times he decided he had to have one in his Artisan's Garden. The Victorians were immensely proud of their potted plants and were keen to display them so that they could be compared with the efforts of their neighbours. The auricula theatre was simply a series of shelves, hung on a wall or fence, on which plants could stand, so called because, surprisingly enough, it was

Cheap galvanized containers can be used to give a dazzling display of colour.

originally designed to house auriculas, which were fashionable plants at the time. I think the fact that they called them theatres says it all – they provided an opportunity to show off and to bring some colour and drama into what, for most, could be a hard and unglamorous world.

CONTAINERS

The Artisan's Garden is graced with some elegant plant containers that would not have looked out of place at the Palace of Versailles. But if you look closely through the bright flowers and luxuriant foliage spilling over the sides you will see that they are in fact nothing but wooden boxes, 'tarted up', as Geoff would say, with some cheap but very cheerful decoration. They are, again, painted blue-grey, although of course you can use any colour you like. Geoff advised, however, that it's better to keep the colours quiet and subdued.

A home-made window box will cheer up the outside of your house and give you a place for plants – even if you have no garden.

The Gentleman's Garden.

The Gentleman's Garden

The Gentleman's Garden was quite a different story from the Artisan's Garden which, with a little loving care, could be 'home-made' by anybody with a modicum of time and skill. The Gentleman's Garden was expensive and more elaborate, although Geoff determined to keep out of his design any hint of pretension, which he hated.

The design began with a central area of an ornamental garden, which could be seen from the house. The remainder of the plot was, like the Artisan's Garden, divided into modules, again the idea being that viewers and readers could juggle these about to fit them into the overall shape of their own plot.

These modules included a 'secret garden' – a small oasis for escape, where one could simply sit and muse. There was a vegetable plot which was dedicated to the 'deep-bed' system to provide greater productivity in a small space (see page 139). Finally there was a small area for fruit containing a greenhouse, which was hexagonal so as to save space.

Geoff felt that most people would not be able to afford this design all at once. It stretched even the mighty BBC budget. So he suggested that it could be built up over a number of years. For example, he built his paths in expensive paviour bricks. But they could be laid with gravel initially and then, when the coffers were full again, the gravel could be mixed with a little dry cement to provide the perfect base for bricks. Likewise the greenhouse, whilst being highly desirable for a keen gardener, is not an absolute necessity at the outset and the outlay could be deferred.

ENCLOSING THE GARDEN
Because a hedge is a far more attractive and dignified boundary for a cottage garden than a fence (provided you have the space) and because the 'Gentleman' was able to afford a more expensive plant, Geoff enclosed the Gentleman's Garden with a hedge of yew, which he always thought to be the emperor of hedging plants. (See page 19 on planting hedges.) It grows to form a dense, dark green background which, when well clipped, has a fine texture you can hardly resist running your hand over. It tends to be slow growing – about 20–25cm (8–10in) a year – but gardeners are patient people and it is wise to wait for the best. If yew is outside the budget, for a similar effect you could use *Thuja plicata*, which will be looser, but will grow about 60cm (2ft) a year.

BRICK PAVING
The paving in the Gentleman's Garden is a real indulgence, because it's

built primarily of paviour bricks which were hand-made, and the edging bricks were moulded with a Tudor rose design. Now that is extravagance, but you can often find second-hand, frost-hardy bricks in demolition yards which would be equally suitable. Don't use house bricks; they'll flake away in no time and look horrible.

Geoff gave me a few good tips about laying bricks. Most are blindingly obvious, but how often have I started on a job and found it much more difficult than it looked, simply because I have not thought it through in the first place?

His first tip was to lay out a few bricks on the soil before you start the job. Then you can measure how wide the path has to be, and you will not have to cut any bricks. Me? I would have laid the concrete base, set the wooden edging into position, laid all the sand and then found my path was too narrow to accommodate the bricks without cutting them.

He then showed me that it is not necessary to use wet cement for the base. Just use an 8:1 mix of ballast and cement, lay it dry and let the soil moisture do the hard work.

His notched levelling board was a good idea. Once he had consolidated the sand by treading it, he levelled it by using the board, with a notch cut at either end so that it could rest on the edging boards, and, by dragging it across the sand towards him, he got a perfectly level surface. Finally he brushed kiln-dried sand into the spaces between the bricks and consolidated them with a vibrating pad, which can be hired from any tool-hire shop.

In the Gentleman's Garden he left out bricks at intervals, to provide planting spaces in which, after he had knocked out the mortar and conditioned the soil with some compost, he planted with low-growing flowering plants and herbs. Geoff chose to do this randomly, but formal designs can be used if preferred.

The difficult part in the Gentleman's Garden was the circle at the intersection of the brick paths. For the centre of the circle he pinched an idea from Edwin Lutyens, Gertrude Jekyll's working partner, who was not a bad gardener in his own right, although I would argue not as good as Geoff. He sank terracotta flower pots of ever-decreasing size into the ground tight up against each other to form concentric circles,

Opposite: This charming row of cottages close to Barnsdale shows how much the cottage garden style enhances the smallest house.

The cleverly designed brick paths and the love seat are the focal point of the Gentleman's Garden.

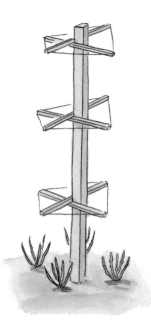

GROWING RASPBERRIES ON A POST

This clever idea for a raspberry column was Geoff's way of saving space and providing an interesting feature in the fruit garden at the same time. Cross timbers are nailed to a post set in the ground and their ends are joined with wire. The wires support bamboo canes, to which the raspberries are trained.

finishing with a small pot set upside down. Then, for the rest of the circle, because the bricks were hand-made and likely to be of slightly differing sizes, he marked circles for each row in the mortar, using a string tied to a central peg. It was necessary to cut some of the bricks, for the inner circles particularly, to a wedge shape, which you can do with a hired angle grinder. The effect was delightful and I am sure that many a visitor has left with their partner insisting, 'That's just what we need, dear.'

Geoff decided to set the small hexagonal greenhouse on a paving base with a paved path to the door.

Geoff was always insistent on getting the levels for this kind of construction exactly right, so his first job, after marking out the area, was to set some pegs out and to level the tops of them with a board and a spirit level. Then he prepared the base with a dry ballast and cement mix and laid each slab on five points of mortar, levelling them to the top of the pegs with a spirit level and the judicious use of the handle of a club hammer to tap the slabs down. He made the circular base for the greenhouse by laying the slabs on the ground, marking a circle with a string tied to a peg and then cutting with an angle grinder.

DIVIDING THE MODULES

To preserve an open structure in the garden and add height Geoff used trellis to divide each module from the other, and two attractive arches at the intersections. Again he went for the expensive option, using hardwood trellis and posts. But here again, cheaper trellis is available and could be used if the bank manager keeps hammering at the door. The arches were fixed first, ensuring that they were positioned exactly over the centre of the path, and then the trellis was fixed to posts each side of the arch and planted with a profusion of sweet-smelling flowering climbers.

THE FRUIT GARDEN

Because there was little space in the Gentleman's Garden, Geoff restricted the fruit surrounding the small greenhouse to fan-trained or espalier trees. They were trained on to wires stretched between posts set in the ground, with straining bolts at either end of the row. Contrary to popular opinion, trained fruit trees are easy to prune and will certainly give you a bumper crop, provided you choose a variety that suits your conditions. I have found Cox very difficult, for example. Old Alfred in the village warned me about this before I planted them, but I did not listen. Now I know better.

The trees were complemented by redcurrants, blackcurrants, standard gooseberries and strawberries. But the idea that I thought was most ingenious was the raspberry column. Raspberries can take up a lot of room if grown in a straight row, so Geoff set a post into the ground, nailed some cross timbers to the top, joined the ends with wire (as illustrated opposite) and used the wire to support bamboo canes on to which the raspberry canes were tied. Grown this way raspberries form a column of fruit which is attractive and easy to manage.

THE PLANTS

Before Geoff did any planting in either garden, he prepared the beds by double-digging (see page 140), following his maxim, 'Get the soil right, and the rest will come right'. Whilst the plants were different in each of the two cottage gardens, the theme was the same in both. It is impossible to mention every plant that Geoff grew, because he was a plantophile and stuffed them into every corner he could find, but here is a brief description of the most important and useful to the cottage gardener.

TREES

Because the two cottage gardens were small they had few trees, as would probably have been the case with the cottage gardens of old. The tree the cottage gardeners would have favoured above all others would have been the apple. With its abundance of pale pink blossom in spring and colourful edible fruits this has to be the choice if your garden is too small for more than one or two trees, as it was for Geoff. In the Gentleman's Garden, in addition to the espaliers and fan-trained trees there is one step-over apple tree that is trained to reach no more than 45cm (18in) in height but bears a considerable crop of fruit for its size.

There are numerous other trees that can be grown in a cottage garden, of course. The basic rule is to keep them small and plant them in places which will not entirely exclude the sun – otherwise you will be limited to growing only shade-loving plants. One of my favourites is the Juneberry, *Amelanchier lamarckii*, which has delicate white flowers in spring, bronze young foliage which turns deep red or yellow in autumn and small black berries which Geoff told me were once used as a substitute for raisins. It looks less dramatic in the summer, so I grow a summer-flowering clematis through it to provide good colour from spring to the onset of winter. This

Betula pendula, a delicate weeping tree with contrasting white bark.

Lathyrus latifolius.

Lathyrus odoratus 'Geoff Hamilton'.

Rosa 'New Dawn'.

can be done with any tree, but avoid very vigorous varieties such as Clematis montana, which will swamp your tree, your house and yourself, if you stand around for too long.

The silver birch, *Betula pendula*, is a superb tree, with its white bark and delicate tracery of branches in winter, but it may be too big for the smaller garden; in which case try the Himalayan birch, *Betula utilis*, which is smaller and has brilliant white, peeling bark. Perhaps the most common tree in the older cottage gardens would have been the May tree or common hawthorn, *Crataegus monogyna*. Grown as a standard to make a rounded crown, it will be covered in exquisite white flowers in spring and scarlet berries in autumn. There are, of course, many other varieties, some with deep pink flowers and all bearing red berries.

CLIMBING PLANTS

Geoff's philosophy was to have none of his walls or fences exposed. He liked to see a dense mass of foliage and flower, a colourful backdrop to set off the rest of the planting, and in the cottage garden particularly he felt the need for it to be scented wherever possible.

Geoff chose climbers that were typical of the cottage garden and, although he used some newer varieties to get good flowering power and disease resistance, he always chose plants that were redolent of bygone days. Typical of the climbers he used were:

Clematis 'Abundance' syn. *C. viticella* 'Abundance': a late-flowering, soft purple variety.

Clematis 'Nelly Moser': an early, large-flowered variety with rose-mauve flowers.

Clematis 'Niobe': deep red flowers with yellow anthers, flowering from July to October.

Lathyrus latifolius: the perennial sweet pea, with small racemes of pink flowers.

Lathyrus odoratus: the annual sweet pea, in various colours, grown from seed in autumn or early spring.

Lonicera x *americana*: a strong-growing climber, yellow-flowered with a flush of purple.

Lonicera x *brownii* 'Dropmore Scarlet': small fragrant red flowers with an orange throat.

Rosa 'Alchymist': a medium-growing, strongly fragrant yellow climbing rose that flowers throughout the summer.

Rosa 'Brother Cadfael': a bushy rambler rose with strongly scented, double globular flowers of soft pink.

Rosa 'Blush Noisette': a short climber of gentle growth, with abundant flowers of blush lilac pink.

Rosa 'New Dawn': a smaller rambler rose with semi-double flowers of soft blush pink.

Rosa 'Madame Caroline Testout': a vigorous climbing rose with lush foliage, deep pink flowers and a very strong perfume.

SHRUBS

Shrubs form the structure of the two cottage gardens, giving them an architectural perspective and forming a foil for the tumultuous colour of the herbaceous plants. Among the varieties Geoff grew were:

Berberis thunbergii 'Atropurpurea Nana': a small rounded bush with reddish-purple foliage.

Deutzia x hybrida 'Magicien': a deciduous shrub with a profusion of pink, white-edged flowers.

Hydrangea heteromalla: a large deciduous shrub with large open heads of white flowers.

Lavandula angustifolia: the Old English lavender, an evergreen shrub with grey-green aromatic foliage and purple-blue flowers.

Potentilla fruticosa 'Daydawn': a long-flowering shrub with an abundance of canary yellow flowers.

Ribes sanguineum: the flowering currant, which bears pink and white flowers before the leaves emerge, when they are complemented by fresh young growth.

Weigela florida: varieties are grown for their radiant red, white or pink, funnel-shaped flowers.

Viburnum tinus: an evergreen plant with white flowers that appear from autumn to early spring.

HERBACEOUS PLANTS

In both gardens Geoff resisted the fashionable idea of 'themed' or 'blended' planting, where flowering plants are planted in drifts of single colours, designed to blend with their neighbours to form a 'harmonized' picture (as advocated by Gertrude Jekyll). The essence of cottage garden planting is chaos. That is what appeals so much to me about it. Chaos I can handle – it is order I find more difficult. And Geoff was just the same. He never, ever worried about clashing colours or 'planting schemes'. The two cottage gardens were planted in just this random way and the result was enchanting. Of the numerous plants Geoff used, these were some of the most important:

Tall plants

Alcea: hollyhocks – biennials or short-lived perennials – have been grown since the sixteenth century and have tall spikes of rosette-like flowers in different colours, appearing in summer or early autumn.

Campanula: a versatile plant with varieties of all heights, which is suitable for most planting conditions. Campanulas can be annuals, biennials or perennials and come in a variety of colours from white

through to deep blue.

Delphinium: has tall spikes of flowers – mainly light or dark blue but they can be pink or white – flowering during summer.

Helenium: late-summer and autumn-flowering perennial with bright yellow, daisy-like flower heads.

Helianthus decapetalus: a tall sunflower with vivid yellow flowers, some of which need no staking.

Lupinus: mainly grown as perennials,

lupins have imposing racemes of flowers in many different colours.

Medium-sized plants

Alchemilla mollis: a plant that will grow almost anywhere and bears sprays of greenish-yellow flowers in summer. Good ground cover.

Aquilegia: a short-lived perennial grown for its comely, spurred flowers in many colours. It will self-seed freely to provide a reliable succession and is comfortable in quite deep shade.

Aster x frikartii 'Mönch': a radiant blue, daisy-like flower appearing in mid-summer to late autumn.

Astilbe: a summer-flowering perennial grown for its delicate panicles of star-shaped flowers in varying shades of pink and white.

Euphorbia: a rounded bush covered in spring flowers of a succulent greenish-yellow.

Geranium pratense: the cranesbill has been grown by cottagers for centuries. Summer flowering, it is semi-evergreen and has attractive cup-shaped flowers in many shades.

Kniphofia: the red hot poker, which has racemes of bright yellow-orange flowers and thick, grass-like leaves.

Osteospermum: an evergreen, semi-woody perennial with bright, daisy-like flowers of many different colours, appearing in summer and autumn.

Papaver nudicaule: one of Geoff's favourite flowers, it has an enormous range of vivid colours and elegant cup-shaped flowers throughout the spring and summer.

Penstemon: a very fashionable plant at present, it bears tubular, nodding flowers

of all shades, flowering in summer and autumn.

Phlox maculata: a summer-flowering plant with a profusion of pink or white flowers borne on strong stems that do not need staking.

Short plants

Aubrieta: a delightful little edging or rock plant that forms mounds of grey-blue foliage with masses of mainly blue flowers in spring.

Dianthus: has semi-double or double flowers often with a strong perfume. It likes full sun.

Diascia: summer- and autumn-flowering annuals and perennials with tubular flowers of varying shades of pink.

Erigeron karvinskianus: a wonderful little plant with daisy-like flowers that change from white, through pink to red and flower all summer. It self-seeds easily and will even seed in walls.

Geum: a low-growing summer-flowering plant, with a wide variety of colours, that forms a clump of bright colour in spring and summer.

Heuchera: grown for its mottled-green and coppery-brown foliage, it often provides a bonus of pale green flowers.

Nepeta x faassenii: catmint has been grown in cottage gardens since 1784. It has blue flowers like lavender and soft grey foliage. It is a favourite haunt of cats who love to lie in it.

Omphalodes cappadocica: this is a lovely little shade-loving plant which will provide blue flowers through the summer.

Primula: again, a huge range of varieties and colours to choose from. Some new, garish varieties have recently been

Euphorbia.

produced, which would not fit comfortably into a cottage garden.

Primula vulgaris: our native primrose, should perhaps be the choice.

Pulmonaria officinalis: the lungwort has been grown in cottage gardens since 1597 because it was thought to cure ailments of the lung. It has superb spotted leaves and pretty pink and blue flowers. A good, reliable shade-lover.

Viola: in a huge range of colours and varieties, this gentle little flower is a must for the cottage garden.

Bulbs

Allium: provides a dramatic show of tiny flowers packed together in a spherical umbel. There are varieties that flower in spring, summer or autumn.

Anemone coronaria: produces red, white or blue daisy-like flowers in early spring.

Crocus: flowers in a wide range of colours in early spring.

Cyclamen hederifolium: a plant that thrives under trees and unfailingly produces a show of lovely pink flowers over marbled grey and green foliage.

Fritillaria meleagris: a magnificent plant that looks as though it should be rare, but is not. It has hanging, bell-shaped flowers that are chequered on the outside in shades of white, maroon, purple, pink and grey.

Galanthus nivalis: the snowdrop is the first bulb to flower, making a cheering sight after winter. It can be lifted, divided and moved whilst still in flower.

Muscari botryoides: the grape hyacinth is another old favourite, giving a splendid display of bright blue flowers.

Narcissus: The daffodil is now produced in a huge variety of sizes and colours. It has the slight disadvantage in the cottage garden that the leaves are unsightly until about six to eight weeks after flowering, when they can be cut down.

Cyclamen hederifolium.

Omphalodes cappadocica.

ANNUALS AND BIENNIALS

Between all this planting Geoff filled every spare space with annuals and biennials — sweet williams, foxgloves, wallflowers, marigolds, clarkia, the annual gypsophila, mignonette, nasturtiums and a whole host of other plants, all grown in his greenhouse. In this way he softened the structure and formality of the shrubs and trees with a tumult of unruly colour, to lift the soul and brighten the weariest spirit.

Geoff was proud of his two cottage gardens and, if you should happen to ask for my opinion, I would say he had every right to be. Whether artisan or gentleman I think I could live happily in either of them. Like all cottage dwellers I know I would be constantly changing the design and moving the plants — but that benign dissatisfaction is the most enduring and comforting aspect of being a genuine cottage gardener. The cottage gardens are now filled each day with an avid public, but there was a time when they were the haven of peace and tranquillity that traditionally the cottage garden has always been: the mainstay of the British countryside and the heart of the old rural economy.

Diascia.

The OK Garden

THE IDEA TAKES SHAPE

The idea for the Ornamental Kitchen Garden, or the OK Garden, as it came to be known, had been mulling around in Geoff's head for a long time. It arose because he had two ideas he wanted to crystallize. The first was his certain knowledge that the majority of his readers and viewers did not have huge gardens with large borders, rolling lawns and walled vegetable plots. They were, by and large, people who lived in modest houses with small gardens, who wanted them to look good but also wanted to grow vegetables to feed a family of voracious kids. They probably felt they had to make a choice – to grow all flowers or all vegetables – because they did not have room for both, or get an allotment, which many people cannot, or do not have time for.

His second idea concerned his passionate desire to conserve the environment and to share that desire with his audience. Before Geoff persuaded me to turn my garden over to organic methods he and I would argue for hours, usually over a pint or two of good Ruddles beer, about the influence that modern farming and commercial horticulture had had on the way that crops were grown in the garden these days. I would argue that without monoculture, pesticides and herbicides we would not have the same quality or quantity of food in the shops, at prices people could afford, while he would argue that these have had an adverse effect on the modern gardener. He reasoned that because the commercial growers and farmers grew in rows, for convenient cultivation, the gardener had followed this line. Because chemicals had been so successful in controlling problems on the farm, gardeners had followed suit, with terrible effects on the environment. We had forgotten that using monoculture and chemicals was not the only way and that we ought to get back to some of the old methods. I used to accuse him of living in the past, but I have to admit that he was not suggesting a return to common grazing land and strip farming. He argued that the huge surpluses that farmers were producing left plenty of room for organic methods in agriculture and he suggested that the resulting produce would demand a considerable premium. I didn't realize how prophetic the old boy could be.

He knew that if a garden was put down entirely to vegetables it would become a fatal attraction for all the pests in the area: breakfast for bugs, lunch for larvae and dinner for dung beetles, with special offers for aphids, carrot fly, onion fly, caterpillars, thrips, slugs and snails – all of whom would bring a friend. But when Geoff thought through the history of the cottage garden he could think of no reference to this kind gardening, with each vegetable grown as a monoculture. In the old days people did not distinguish between different types of plant. They just grew them all together, looking at some, eating others, curing ailments and making perfumes and dyes from yet more. They were successful because they hid their treasures away amongst all kinds of other plants, so deceiving the bugs with artifice.

Geoff was also concerned about the new vegetable varieties that have been developed by plant breeders for the retail market. In order to maximise their profits, and to produce vegetables that persuade shoppers to buy and so suit supermarkets, they have aimed at high yield, conformity of shape and good colour – because if it looks good people will buy. Scant attention seems to have been paid to flavour, yet surely that is a pretty important quality in the food we buy.

Geoff did not condemn new varieties out of hand. One of the other important things the plant breeders have been doing is breed varieties that are resistant to pests and diseases, which reduce the need for chemical control, and that, he felt, had to be good. But he still felt sure that a return to some of the older, more flavoursome varieties, as well as to some of the old methods, would be beneficial.

So he set out to reproduce a garden that embraced all the ideas of the gardeners of a hundred years ago, embodying the old wisdom gained through the painful process of survival, and brought up to date to suit the needs, tastes and the pocket of the modern gardener.

THE BASIC APPROACH

Geoff's first inclination was to wind his brain back about a hundred years to look at the way it used to be done.

He would garden organically (see pages 27–57) as gardeners of old did, and he would grow really strong plants, of disease-resistant varieties where possible, which could withstand a small attack of pests or diseases, and he would hide his vegetables by growing them in small patches amongst his flowering plants, to ward off insect pests. These seek out their prey by sight or smell, so if you can disguise them both you will confuse the hell out of them. At the same time the flowers will protect the crops by providing a habitat for all the good and friendly predators I discussed on page 47.

He would even do it with crops like potatoes, which everybody generally believes must be grown in straight rows so that they can be easily earthed up and harvested. He told me of a wonderful old lady gardener he met, who lived in the country and grew all her vegetables in this way. She

had a habit of popping a seed potato into any small space in her garden as soon as it became free, right through the spring and summer, and as a result she had a small crop of fresh new potatoes all the time. Incidentally, if you draw some short drills in a sunny spot and sow some lettuce, radish, beetroot, spring onion or any other successional crops, and do the same two or three weeks later, you'll never be short of salad.

The vegetables would not spoil the borders but would be made to compliment them, using some of the many crops that will really enhance the look of your garden, like red cabbage, ruby chard, sweet corn, globe artichokes as well as all the fruit crops (more on that in the next chapter). In this way the OK Garden would work with nature to produce food for a family as well as food for the gardener's soul.

Neat, mellow paths, overhung with radiant planting, are a feature of Geoff's Ornamental Kitchen Garden.

121

The small circular lawn in the OK Garden is surrounded by mixed planting of flowers, herbs and vegetables.

The OK Garden

The Ornamental Kitchen Garden was to be 9m x 15m (30ft x 50ft), which is probably a little larger than the modern estate plot, but not a lot. In designing a garden there is always a temptation to let one's imagination run riot and fill it with all sorts of features that will compete with each other for space and the attention of the eye. This is a serious trap with any small garden, but with an ornamental kitchen garden it is even more important to avoid falling into it, because the thing you need most is growing space. One of the hard lessons that Geoff learned during his landscaping career was that garden designs should be carefully thought out and measured, and kept as simple as possible — particularly if the garden is small; paths, lawn, arbours, ponds, etc. should be kept small or kept out.

GEOFF'S DESIGNER PATIO

The patio figured large in Geoff's design. This was partly because he worked very hard and he really valued his relaxation time, which he spent outside if possible, preferably with Lynda and preferably with a large glass of the old red biddy in his hand (preferably my red biddy). And it was partly because his patio also doubled as a sunny place to put his cold frame and as a standing-out ground for developing plants.

He built the patio from reconstituted stone paving, which is attractive and much cheaper than the real thing. But in the design he came up against a problem. Because paving is square, unless you do something special you will end up with a square or rectangular patio, which is unattractive and tends to cut the garden in half. Most builders do this, using concrete slabs, and it looks terrible. Geoff solved this problem by cutting a tiny circular lawn into his patio, cutting the paving with an angle grinder to make the circle he needed. He also left some planting spaces near the fence to provide space for planting trees and climbers that would eventually cover it.

A lawn is something of an indulgence that needs to be thought about carefully. It takes up space that could be used for growing and, however small, it will need to be cut once a week. So you will have to invest in a small mower and a pair of edging shears. On the other hand, it will provide you with some good composting material, essential for strong plants, it looks good and it will help to attract wildlife. So think on.

FOLLOW THE RED-BRICK ROAD

The main path was designed to be a strong feature, the structural

1   Compost bin
2   Concrete base
3   Planting (mixed herbs and vegetables)
4   Rose arbour
5   Glasshouse
6   Pergola
7   Lollipop apple
8   Early border
9   Mulberry *(Morus nigra)*
10 Planting (mixed flowers, herbs and vegetables)
11 Brick path
12 Planting in gravel in stepping-stone path
13 *Malus* 'John Downie'
14 Lawn
15 Fig
16 Random paving
17 Cobbles with planting
18 Pool
19 Pot
20 Fan-trained fruit

A small corner of the OK Garden showing how well the planting is offset by the brick paths.

123

This kind of family garden will not only provide peace and beauty for the adults, but feed the ravenous hordes as well.

centrepiece for the whole garden. So Geoff splashed out and built it with red paviour bricks, which would look good and withstand frost and wear. There are, of course, cheaper materials he could have used, but he felt that this was the feature that would give shape and form to the garden and the paviour bricks were therefore worth the money. When designing a garden it is sensible to decide early on what kind of budget you have for the hard landscaping and steel yourself to go for the best you can afford, because while it is possible to change from, say, harsh concrete paving to mellow red brick, it is difficult and more expensive in the long term. Most people end up economizing and regret it always. As you can see from the plan, the path led from the patio at the house end of the garden and wound its way in pleasing curves to a rose arbour at the other end.

Geoff still needed other paths to give access to a tightly planted garden, so he put one down the length of each side and another diagonally, crossing the main brick path. These he built from stepping stones made from 45cm (18in) slabs, set about 7.5cm (3in) apart, with pea shingle in between, giving sufficient space to plant small spreading plants between the slabs which would gradually soften the path. If you use sweet-smelling plants such as thyme in this way you will get delicious wafts of perfume when you walk along the path.

While there was now good access to the side borders, which were only 60cm (2ft) wide and easily reached, this was not true of the central beds. So in these Geoff installed strategically placed stepping stones. Placed as the initial planting was done so that they could be put in the most convenient place, these were made from wooden logs set on end, to avoid too much consolidation of the soil by treading. This is important in this type of garden because you will not get much opportunity for deep cultivation, so it is best to dig the soil really well before you plant and then not tread on it at all, if possible.

GEOFF'S TRIUMPHAL ARCH
A pergola, built in the way described opposite, straddled the brick path at the end furthest from the house. It was built because the plot, like many

small garden plots, was flat and uninteresting and the pergola, which was to be clothed with plants, would serve to raise the perspective of the garden. This can partly be done with trees, of course, but trees have the disadvantage of shading large parts of the garden, whilst pergola plants shade only the path beneath it. That is not to say that there were no trees in Geoff's garden, but they were small and, as in the cottage gardens, strategically placed so that they did not cast too much shadow.

The pergola was planted with ornamental climbers such as clematis. Geoff was careful not to choose clematis varieties that would grow too strongly and soon dominate a small garden. So he avoided *Clematis montana* and *C. tangutica* in favour of *C. viticella* and *C. alpina*. The pergola also provided a place to plant runner beans, which scrambled over the top of the structure and hung temptingly down, adding interest and a touch of humour to the garden. He even planted marrows and squashes, tying them into the supports, with the fruits, when they were big enough, supported in netting bags. This is actually quite a difficult way to grow marrows and you may prefer to grow them in the border, where they will make a stunning ornamental plant, but if you have the patience, growing them upwards will undoubtedly save you lots of space that can be used for other things.

Amongst the other decorative climbers he used were monkshood,

MAKING A PERGOLA

Set the posts (made from 7.5 x 7.5cm (3 x 3in) fence posts) into the ground, making sure they are upright, with a spirit level, and straight, with a line. Fix the side rails (made from 4 x 7.5cm (1 ¹/₂in x 3 in) timber) into notches cut into the top of the post and fasten with a coach-bolt. Screw the cross rails to the side rails at 30cm (1ft) intervals using angle brackets. Note the cross rails are shaped to make them more attractive. Finally prepare the soil and plant with climbers, tied to the posts with soft string.

Clematis *'Polish Spirit'.*

Aconitum hemsleyanum, a glorious herbaceous perennial with bright blue flowers that die back in winter, only to re-emerge in triumph in the warmth of the spring; *Actidinia deliciosa*, which has scarlet shoots and white flowers, and gives an exotic touch; and, of course, roses to impart the cottage garden character. The blue passion flower *Passiflora caerulea* appealed to his romantic nature and the tender *Rhodochiton atrosanguineum* with dazzling blue, white and pink flowers tickled his irrepressible sense of fun. Sweet peas had their place as well, and these he would cut and present to Lynda, to fill the house with perfume.

THE ROSE ARBOUR

Although the rose arbour was right at the end of the garden it was at the heart of the design, approached by the generous curve of the brick path and a journey through the magical, highly scented pergola. Here Geoff's extravagant fancy got the better of him. After only a year the rose arbour had become a bower of vivid flower and perfume — a tiny utopia for relaxation and thought. Geoff's quota of thinking and relaxing climbed significantly after its completion. If I went up to see Geoff at Barnsdale in the evening and found nobody at home I would head straight for his beloved arbour, and sure enough ...

His arbour was octagonal, because an octagon is an interesting shape that gives a little more sparkle to the garden. It is not difficult to make, but Geoff would always suggest that people should not try to extend themselves beyond their skills, and if a square was all that could be managed, well, it would soon be covered in plants and nobody would notice the difference.

Now it is my painful duty to expose Geoff as an indulgent old devil who never spent one pound when ten would do. He went out and, once again, spent more money than he had, this time on a sensational seat of an Edwin Lutyens design to put into his arbour.

The planting of the rose arbour was similar to that of the pergola, but he supplemented the climbers he used there with plants like an ornamental vine, *Vitis coignetiae*, which makes splendid, vigorous growth, with leaves that turn bright shades of crimson and purple in autumn. He used a plant closely related to the nasturtium, *Tropaeolum tuberosum*, which has bright foliage and masses of orange-scarlet flowers. *Celastrus orbiculatus* was a particular favourite because in autumn its foliage turns a brilliant yellow and it has brown fruits which split open to reveal glowing red seeds.

And, of course, what better plants to grow on a rose arbour but roses? In this case, because the arbour was small, Geoff chose to plant climbers rather than ramblers. Ramblers climb higher, but they tend to be more

Opposite: A well-planted pergola assaults the senses with colour and perfume.

Hexagonal greenhouses are ideal for the small garden.

rampant and generally flower once or perhaps twice in the season. Climbing roses, on the other hand are, like Geoff, more restrained and, unlike Geoff, flower continuously through the summer. He was careful to use varieties that are resistant to disease, particularly black spot, mildew and rust, as there is no really effective organic control; even insecticidal soap, which is sold as a control for fungal diseases, is rarely completely effective, so the best way to combat disease is through a vigorous, healthy plant. He chose varieties such as *Rosa* 'Noisette Carnée' (syn. *R.* 'Blush Noisette'), which has profuse clusters of double flowers, and is strongly fragrant, starting white and fading to pink; and *R.* 'Guinée', a vigorous rose, suitable for a north-facing aspect, with velvety scarlet flowers borne almost continuously during summer. One of his great favourites was *R.*

'Compassion', with its glorious double pink to apricot flowers which, if given a southern aspect, will flower all summer.

THE ORGANIC OASIS

No organic garden is complete without a pond, because it will be a magnet for wildlife which will march to war on your pests, but it does not have to be big (see page 47). In my garden I have a tiny pond made from a half-barrel and planted with a couple of small water plants. It is always a home for frogs, toads and myriad insects, and we watch birds drinking at it, sometimes accompanied by a very shy hedgehog and a cheeky squirrel. I am waiting for a wildebeest to appear, but no luck so far. Geoff's pond in the OK Garden was also made from a half-barrel and it was extremely upsetting to see how much better it looked than mine. You don't need to tell me anything about sibling rivalry. With the lawn at one side and a few large pebbles placed around, the pond looked as though it had been there all the time.

GEOFF WHERE HE BELONGS – IN THE GLASSHOUSE

For the greenhouse Geoff chose a hexagonal design, because he thought it had a pleasing aesthetic effect in such a small garden, in cedar, because cedar requires little maintenance.

He also made yet another cold frame, to the design shown on page 81, because he clearly needed somewhere to harden off the plants he had grown. A cold frame is a fairly portable structure and Geoff believed that you should be flexible about siting it. So in spring he put it on the patio, because it faced south and would get good sunlight, but in early summer he moved it to a slightly more shady spot where melons and cucumbers would feel more comfortable.

Behind the greenhouse, where it was largely hidden from view, he concreted a small area, because every garden needs a utility area for mixing compost, putting up a potting bench, siting compost bins and storing all the odd bits and pieces you tend to accumulate along the way.

THE PLANT CONTAINERS

There was just a hint of (self-confessed) snobbery about Geoff's views on containers. He hated plastic. He felt that every container, particularly in a small garden, had to earn its aesthetic keep. It should be like a piece of statuary: beautiful in its own right, even when empty.

He did concede that there were a lot of very good plastic containers on the market, but he much preferred containers in terracotta, stone or wood. Like many others, he had to start with plastic containers because he

could not afford anything else, but as soon as he had made a few bob he was off looking for something really beautiful to replace them. He even grew his tomatoes, cucumbers, etc. in the greenhouse in hand-thrown terracotta pots – not because they are better for the plants, but because he liked to look at them.

Incidentally, if you do buy terracotta containers for use outside, make sure they are frost proof or else use them only for tender plants and bring them inside in the winter. I can tell you from personal experience of the devastating disappointment of going out on a frosty morning to find expensive containers cracked and useless. And we had brought ours all the way from Italy. Yes, Geoff, I know I should have listened!

'Tumbler' tomatoes, peppers, courgettes, cucumbers and aubergines all grown in containers.

THE PLANTING PLAN

Much of Geoff's planting in the OK Garden was based on annuals, sown or planted in small drifts and removed after flowering. This concept gives the flexibility you need to interplant with vegetables whenever a suitable space arises and to hide them away from predators. But there was still a place for more permanent plants – trees, shrubs and herbaceous perennials.

As I said earlier, the site for these needs to be carefully chosen, but remember that even large plants are quite amenable to a move in the first couple of years, and herbaceous plants can be moved at any stage of growth, from late autumn to early spring, so you do not have to get everything right first time.

TREES

The starting point of any garden should be the trees. Be careful to choose trees of a height and spread to suit the size of the garden. For his OK Garden, apart from the fruit, which was all fan-trained, espalier or step-over varieties, Geoff chose only three trees, all small and productive. The first was a crab apple, *Malus* 'John Downie', which he chose because the fruits are edible and sweet – excellent for making wine and jelly. It has a great profusion of white flowers in spring and large bright orange and red fruits.

The second was a mulberry, *Morus nigra*, which may be too big for some gardens, but he was tempted by it because of its three-fold attraction: deep green leaves, tiny flowers borne in yellow catkins in May and June, and dark red, edible fruits which ripen in August/September.

His final choice was a masterstroke. It was a standard apple tree with the four main branches trained around two hoops to give a formal, rounded head, which Geoff called a 'lollipop' tree. When a tree is trained this way, the hoops are initially supported by canes but these can be removed, along with the hoops, after the first year when the tree will have grown sufficiently for the main branches to be tied in at the top. Eventually it will fill out to give a dense globe of leaf, flowers and then, of course, fruit.

The fruit Geoff grew in the OK Garden was designed to give a good variety of taste and type – peach, nectarine, apricot and fig on the south-facing fence, and trained apples on the west fence, with step-over varieties fronting the border beneath, trained pears and cherries on the other walls and standard gooseberries, raspberries and strawberries in the borders.

Potentilla fruticosa.

SHRUBS

Of course any shrubs could be grown in the borders but Geoff advised some restraint. He pointed out that shrubs have a nasty habit of growing, so choose a few, small varieties, leaving room for the herbaceous and annual plants that would form the main bulk of the planting – as well as space for the vegetables.

The shrubs that Geoff used for the sunny parts of the OK Garden were:

Fuchsia 'Thalia'.

Berberis thunbergii 'Red Chief': has arching branches covered with dark red foliage, yellow flowers in spring and red berries in autumn.

Caryopteris x *clandonensis*: Geoff loved this plant because it forms a mound of grey foliage and carries blue flowers in September/October, just when things are beginning to look dull.

Olearia x *haastii*: a rounded bush about 1.25m (4ft) high with white, highly scented flowers in July and August.

Paeonia suffruticosa: the tree peony, an exotic plant with stunning foliage and a mass of flowers that vary with the variety, from white with a yellow centre, to vivid scarlet and deep pink.

Potentilla fruticosa: produces bright yellow flowers on and on through late spring and summer.

Spiraea x *bumalda* 'Goldflame': a plant that delighted Geoff because of its bright golden foliage in spring, followed by large, flat clusters of carmine flowers, which last from July to September.

Teucrium x *lucidrys*: a low-growing alpine plant which Geoff valued for its dark green foliage with grey beneath, and deep pink flowers whose lower lips are spotted with red and white.

Fuchsia: Geoff also grew hardy fuchsias in this part of the garden for their delicate pendulous flowers, which give colour and shape right through the summer.

Mahonia media 'Charity'.

Butterflies on *Sedum spectabile* 'Meteor'.

In the shadier parts of the garden he used:

Aucuba japonica: the spotted laurel, an evergreen shrub with waxy green leaves splashed with gold.

Fatsia japonica: this is usually grown as a house plant but will survive quite well in a sheltered spot. It is an evergreen with glossy, palm-like leaves and Geoff revelled in its exotic appearance.

Hydrangea species: Geoff grew *H. chinensis* 'Grayswood', which has flowers of a blue-pink centre surrounded by white florets which change to red later in the year, but there are many others to choose from.

Mahonia x *media* 'Charity': an attractive, holly-like evergreen with sprays of scented yellow flowers in winter.

Photinia x *fraseri* 'Red Robin': this outstanding New Zealand introduction was one of Geoff's favourites because it is an evergreen with striking red young foliage which, if pruned back when it turns green, will produce new young red growths.

Skimmia japonica subsp. *reevesiana* 'Rubella': an evergreen that carries bright red buds through the winter which open to form white, scented flowers with yellow anthers.

HARDY PERENNIALS

Because the OK Garden was essentially a cottage garden Geoff grew similar perennials to those he grew in the two cottage gardens – the Artisan's Garden and the Gentleman's Garden, albeit that the OK Garden preceded them chronologically. However, Geoff never did the same thing twice, so there were some variations.

For the sunny parts of the garden he chose:

Acanthus spinosus: a stately perennial, producing many spikes of mauve and white flowers, which Geoff chose as a striking backcloth for the border.

Agapanthus 'Bressingham Blue', a bulb which has grassy foliage topped by large heads of pendulous blue flowers in late summer.

Anchusa azurea 'Loddon Royalist': an old favourite with cottage gardeners, and therefore with Geoff, forming flowers of deep blue, like giant forget-me-nots.

Aster novae-angliae: one of the more disease-resistant varieties of Michaelmas daisies. Geoff used this to help him to stick to his organic guns and avoid mildew the non-chemical way. It produces daisy-like flowers of lavender-blue in late summer.

Campanula lactiflora: a plant Geoff valued because it readily self-seeds, and presents bell-shaped blue or white flowers in spring and early summer.

Centaurea dealbata: the cornflower – a plant that is easy to grow and will provide blue blooms for most of the summer.

Coreopsis verticillata: another easily grown plant which will produce striking yellow flowers through the summer and into early autumn.

Delphinium species: Geoff loved delphiniums, one of the classic country garden plants, which bear fine spikes of beautiful flowers of all shades of blue through to white.

Echinacea purpurea: this was once called – and is similar to – rudbeckia and was one of Geoff's all-time favourites, producing purple, daisy-like flowers from June to the end of September.

Echinops ritro: Geoff used the globe thistle, with grey, jagged foliage and steely blue, spherical flower heads, to provide a dramatic touch and as a foil to the bright colours surrounding it.

Euphorbia: will grow in sun or shade. Geoff used *E. characias* subsp. *wulfenii* Margery Fish Group, a handsome evergreen with bright spikes of yellow flowers.

Hemerocallis 'Bejewelled': Geoff used this for its free-flowering habit and arching light green foliage.

Lavatera 'Barnsley': Geoff planted the mallow for its dependable profusion of pink flowers from June to the end of September.

Lilium 'Enchantment': he admired this for its lovely, upward-facing orange-red trumpets with black-spotted throats.

Penstemon: perhaps the plant Geoff loved most, for its profusion of bell-shaped flowers, ranging from purple, through red and pink, to white.

Phygelius x *rectus* 'African Queen': a plant that resembles a fuchsia but has a great abundance of long, narrow, pink trumpets with yellow throats.

Pleioblastus auricomus: a slow-spreading bamboo which Geoff chose for its purple stems and broad, yellow leaves with bright green stripes.

Monarda didyma: better known as bergamot, this resembles sage, bearing hooded flowers from June to September.

Nectaroscordum siculum subsp. *bulgaricum*: a plant that Geoff felt had truly earned its current popularity, having large bell-shaped heads of pendulous green flowers tinged with purple.

Polygonum amplexicaule: this can be an invasive plant and needs to be kept in check, but Geoff chose it for its good ground-cover properties and wonderful spikes of pink flowers in summer.

Sedum spectabile 'Brilliant': he used this to add colour to the border in late summer and autumn. With large, fleshy leaves and great clusters of small red flowers it arrives at just the right time to give a splash of colour when the plants around it are fading.

Sidalcea 'Party Girl': chosen to brighten a corner with its buttercup-like leaves and bright pink flowers.

Euphorbia characias
subsp. *wulfenii*
'Lambrook Gold'.

Opposite Geoff's predilection for dense planting resulted in a wonderful show of colour and foliage.

Geoff was never daunted by shady areas in his garden, and he always seemed to find something interesting and impressive to fill them. For the OK Garden he chose firstly quite a few ferns of one sort or another. The land was heavy and tended to be moist, so they thrived in these conditions and provided an exquisite background for the other plants, which included:

Astilbe 'Köln': requires a damp position in the front of the border. It has pink flowers which are followed by attractive seed heads.

Epimedium grandiflorum 'Rose Queen': a favourite ground-cover plant of Geoff's, with racemes of pendulous, long-spurred, lilac flowers, offset by dark brownish-red young leaves.

Helleborus niger: the Christmas rose. Geoff could often be seen, if you crept up quietly, gently lifting the flower heads to admire the rich, dark interiors of the saucer-shaped greenish-white flowers.

Hosta species: Geoff loved hostas but was particularly wary about attack from slugs, so he surrounded them liberally with chipped bark, which went some way to preventing damage.

Pulmonaria officinalis Cambridge Blue Group: Geoff would never be without a lungwort. He seemed to be lost without them. Lovely leaves, spotted with white and silver, and flowers of red, pink and white really do demand that this plant occupies a place in the shady border.

Epimedium grandiflorum 'Rose Queen' and *Geranium macrorrhizum*.

THE ANNUALS

The plants described above probably sound like a lot for a fairly small plot, and it has to be said that Geoff did like to cram his plants in close together, to provide a really good display all through the year. By pruning and trimming he kept them in check and he still had lots of space for annuals, which he loved for their optimism and vibrant colour.

The hardy annuals he chose were anchusa, because it attracts bees, the marigold, calendula, because its yellow flowers lifted his spirits, clarkia, an old favourite with superb double flowers of red, pink and white, and *Convolvulus minor*, which has a profusion of trumpet-shaped flowers, which attract hoverflies by the thousand. Amongst these he planted the poached egg plant, *Limnanthes douglasii*, and of course nasturtiums, a cottage garden favourite. Obviously he could not be without sweet peas, which he grew through his small trees, trailed over fences and on 'wigwams' of canes.

The half-hardy department was packed with variety. Ageratum at the front, antirrhinums and asters lording it at the back, begonias, cinerarias, cosmos, impatiens and a whole

A wonderful example of
how well the shapes
and colours of flowers
and vegetables
complement each other.

regiment of others, not fighting with each other for attention but together forming a tapestry of colour, like a Monet painting.

THE VEGETABLE HOT-POT

On its own the OK Garden would have been a dazzling garden, but add the vegetables and it became something else altogether. What Geoff was aiming for in the OK Garden was a succession of vegetables that would make even the small gardener more or less self-sufficient throughout the year. He recognized, of course, that some gardens would be so small that this was not possible; you can't get a quart out of a pint pot. But most 'estate'-sized gardens do have sufficient room if the process is well planned – and what a delight to be able to pick your own fresh vegetables half an hour before they're cooked.

So first he suggested avoiding those crops which could be more easily and cheaply grown commercially, like maincrop potatoes, which take up a lot of space and are no better, unless you are resolute about avoiding chemicals. Nevertheless he liked to grow a few earlies because of their mouthwatering taste. Peas are another space-hungry crop that you can almost equal in a supermarket, although Geoff would not be without some mangetout.

Geoff seemed to have the happy knack of being able to extend the growing season right through the year. He started with plants grown in the greenhouse, in growing bags or directly into the soil. These were mainly salad crops, which mature quite happily inside. When his greenhouse began to overflow he would make use of his cloches and his frame. Planting in cloches and frames, which are cooler than a greenhouse, tends to slow the growing process a little, but nevertheless the plants should be OK.

In early February he would sow crops for growing under small lantern cloches in his borders – lettuce, radish, spring onion, baby carrots, turnips, cabbage, cauliflowers, spinach, onions and beetroot. These would be multiple-seeded (see page 146) and usually planted out three or four weeks after sowing, depending on the season. The cloches would be removed during the day if the weather was warm and dispensed with altogether as soon as the risk of frost was over. This was often quite early, around the beginning or middle of May, because if frost threatened to return the cloches could easily be replaced. From then onwards it was simply a matter of remembering (not Geoff's strong point) to sow the same crops for succession, in the open, every two or three weeks until they were replaced by maincrop varieties. If he did forget and ran out of lettuce, for example, I would always take one to him, saying that I understood that he was unable to maintain his succession, and would he like one of mine to tide him over? Well, one has to get one's pleasures where one can!

The next phase, which started in late February or early March, was aimed at crops that were to mature a little later. Outdoor tomatoes, cucumbers, courgettes and marrows, beans of all kinds, sweet corn and squashes would eventually be jostling for space amongst his flowers, all nestling within a protective cover that would knock the best Paris fashion houses into a cocked hat and all anxious to provide succulent meals throughout the year.

Before doing any of this he had devised a list of vegetables that were not only suited to this kind of growing system but met his criteria. The first priority was taste and Geoff only recommended vegetables that he reckoned still tasted like they did when he was a boy. The second priority was disease resistance (see page 48), because Geoff was determined that no chemicals would ever contaminate his vegetables again. The third priority was, of course, the beauty of the plant, and there are a lot of very beautiful plants to choose from. For example, it was Geoff who first introduced me to ruby chard, a dazzling plant with deep red leaves which tastes just as good as ordinary chard or spinach. Beetroot was another of his favourites, because of its vibrant red leaves. He grew beetroot multiple seeded so that the seedlings pushed each other apart as they grew and delivered the most delicious small roots. Red cabbage, with its great ball of purple leaves, was also prominent on Geoff's list. But the plant he would really show off about was the globe artichoke. Grown at the back of the border it would stand in stately splendour, with its grey, spiky foliage and huge pinkish heads. Geoff and I would often sit in his garden, each with one of his artichoke heads, sharing a bowl of vinaigrette and a bottle of red wine. Bliss!

With its decorative combination of flowers and vegetables, Geoff's OK Garden was such that anyone who used it as inspiration for their own garden would soon be replete with good, cheap food that they could enjoy in the kind of paradise that Geoff built for himself.

Florence fennel not only makes a wonderful foliage plant but also supplies a delicious vegetable to the discerning cook.

Food, glorious food

GEOFF'S SLOW-FOOD OUTLET

Geoff could never think of growing vegetables just to fill bellies. Whilst it is true that he filled multiple bellies – visitors to Barnsdale rarely left without an armful of vegetables, which must have brought the greengrocery trade in Oakham close to bankruptcy – that was by no means all Geoff got out of growing his veg. It gave him the sublime pleasure of carrying an overflowing basket into the kitchen, in the certain knowledge that they would provide a culinary experience that would ravish his taste buds. He derived a deep sense of security from knowing that he had a shed full of stored fruit and vegetables that would last through the winter – a primeval kind of feeling that he could not explain. He also saw great beauty in a well-tended vegetable garden, with a wide variety of productive plants.

THE VEGETABLE GARDEN AT BARNSDALE

The vegetable plot at Barnsdale was big – almost an acre – because Geoff used it for trials and for demonstration areas for *Gardeners' World*. He also had a number of smaller areas where specific methods could be demonstrated, so they had to be similar to the kind of plot the average viewer would have. I do not intend here to go into the cultural details of every kind of vegetable that Geoff grew, but propose to describe some of his philosophies and inventions and the methods he used himself and recommended to others.

Geoff's basic platform for vegetable gardening was, as ever, a directly practical one which, as I have explained earlier, started with getting the soil into rich and nutritious condition by incorporating lots of good organic matter, and included conducting a sensible rotation plan to keep disease at bay, intercropping to keep the land occupied and productive and, most importantly to Geoff, not smothering it with chemicals to kill everything in sight (see pages 27–57). But he also used some special approaches that he had tried and tested over many years and had found to be good.

DIGGING DEEP

The deep-bed system of cultivation for vegetables was not invented by Geoff, but he was one of the early experimenters with it and he discovered that by using it he could get much higher yields per square yard than by any other method. After all, when you grow plants in rows in a conventional bed it must be true that at least half your land is put down to

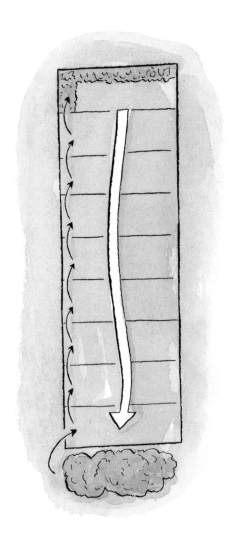

DOUBLE DIGGING

Dig a trench at the top of the plot and wheel the soil down to the bottom. Fork over the bottom of the trench, incorporating organic matter. Dig the second trench, throwing the soil into the first. Fill the final trench with the soil originally taken from the first. Make sure the manure is spread evenly, so that it's incorporated from top to bottom.

paths, but the deep-bed system avoids this. Additionally in a deep bed it is easier to provide a really high level of fertility, which will enable you to plant much more intensively and thus get more vegetables to fill the larder.

Geoff started a deep bed by marking out a strip of land, 1.25m (4ft) wide, which is a sensible distance so that you can reach across it from either side. His golden rule was that, once dug, the beds were never, never, never trodden on, so it was of fundamental importance that they were easily accessible.

Next he began digging, in this case double digging, incorporating plenty of compost, animal manure or spent mushroom compost, to provide really good drainage and enable deep root penetration, to lighten and aerate the soil as well as improve fertility. This is hard work, but take heart from the fact that it will not have to be done often. Geoff recommended double digging once every four or five years, but I confess that I have flagrantly flouted the master's advice and have not re-dug my deep beds in fourteen years, and they are still producing magnificent crops. Mind you, my soil is light and I do single dig them – that is, dig as for double-digging but to only one spade depth – every year, including cow muck or garden compost, to give them renewed vitality.

The deep beds at Barnsdale are edged with timber to keep them tidy. This is not essential, though it is useful if you are a tidy-minded kind of person. You will find that when you cultivate or weed the soil tends to slide on to the path, and a wooden edging will prevent this.

I was frequently delighted by Geoff's simple but truly elegant solutions to the problems he ran up against, and one day, when I went to see him at Barnsdale, I was knocked out by one. I loved my deep beds and swore I would always be wedded to them, but one thing I found irksome was the fact that every time I had sown half a row of seeds I had to walk the whole length of a long bed to sow the other half from the other side. Geoff solved this with a little bridge he made to span the bed, enabling him to get quickly from one side to the other. He knocked it up simply, using the 'rough woodworking' skills our dad had taught us, from half a scaffold plank and four legs braced with 7cm x 2.5cm (3in x 1in) timber. He stapled a piece of rope from one side of the bridge to the other, so that he could easily move it and, as he said, 'Bob's your uncle.'

He generally made his first plantings in March, with plants grown in modules, pots or trays in the greenhouse. When planting this early it is necessary to protect the plants with cloches and Geoff used the ingenious device described on page 82. The plants were planted in blocks, in staggered stations rather than rows, to save on planting space, and the planting distance was usually about two thirds of the normal distance. He made himself a planting board of 7cm x 2cm (3in x $^3/_4$in) timber, with a scale marked off in 15cm (6in) steps so that he could easily measure planting distances.

Another neat trick Geoff showed me was how to draw a perfectly straight row for sowing seeds. He just used the edge of his planting board, pressing it into the soil and moving it backwards and forwards. Such a simple idea, which I would not have thought of, but which has saved me lots of time and has made my deep beds look neat and orderly.

If you have a small garden and some hungry mouths to feed there is no doubt that the deep-bed method will enable you to grow vegetables with less trouble and much more control than by the conventional method, provided you choose the right crops to grow. If you are limited for space Geoff's advice would have been to grow only the things that you cannot buy fresh and wholesome in the supermarket. Lettuce, radish, spring onions, spinach, carrots, beetroot and turnips all fit into this category and are well suited to the deep-bed method.

Other crops that can be grown on deep beds are peas (Geoff recommended the 'leafless' varieties, which do not need supporting), onions, shallots, kohl rabi, chicory, endive, rocket, Chinese cabbage, pak choi and all the herbs. In fact, it is probably true to say that almost anything can be grown on a deep bed, but some crops are better adapted to the firmer soil conditions of a conventional bed – such as main crop brassicas, although early and late varieties are perfectly happy.

Top: Chicory will stand a frost and can stay in the ground until needed.

Above: Rocket makes a spicy addition to winter salads.

The Allotment

Geoff developed a very special vegetable garden at Barnsdale which he called the Allotment, partly because that was the way he presented it on television, but mainly because he loved the whole idea of the allotment culture and did a lot of publicity work to try to preserve it. He would be beside himself with rage if he heard about a plan to close down an area of allotments, particularly if it was being done in order to build 'executive homes'. He saw this as robbing the poor to pay the rich and he would not stand for that in any circumstances. Out would come his trusty word processor again and he would write one (or more) of his many press articles, write to the council concerned or prepare a piece for television.

He did not believe so strongly in the allotment just because he knew what satisfaction and joy could be derived by ordinary people like him from growing good food for your family. This was, of course, a powerful reason, but he also saw the allotment as an important element of the social fabric of a community. It was one of the few places where young and old, from all walks of life, could mix, exchange ideas, swap seeds, plants and vegetables, and become friends with each other. It had a lot of the benefits of the rural village way of life as it used to be, when everybody knew everybody else and you learned respect for each other through working and living together.

I used to be fascinated by Geoff's stories of discussions he had had with allotment holders and other vegetable growers. People like George Flack, who was eighty odd when they met at his lovely cottage in Norfolk. George was a kind, gentle man with a love of his plants so great that his eyes shone with delight when he talked about them. He did all his own work and still dug his big vegetable garden by hand – 'Always with a spade. You can't beat a spade. Don't you try and do that with a fork, master. That just won't work.' He died just before Geoff, so I do hope they met up on the great allotment in the sky. They would be the best of friends, and growing marrows like submarines.

UNUSUAL VEGETABLES

Once, having read one of the more exotic seed catalogues, I asked Geoff why he did not grow more of the unusual vegetables. He gave me a wry little grin, which always heralded one of his quirky little homilies, and said, 'Why do you think they're unusual?' What he meant was that they are often unusual because they are, by and large, rather on the nasty side. However, this does not apply to all. There are vegetables that seem to be overlooked by a lot of gardeners simply, I think, because they are unusual.

Opposite: Geoff's Allotment demonstrates what can be done to feed the family on even a small piece of ground.

George Flack, a gardener much admired by Geoff, working in his productive Norfolk garden, aged over eighty.

Geoff used to sing their praises because they are easy to grow, mostly easy to store and delicious to eat. They are:

Roots

JERUSALEM ARTICHOKES: these should be planted in a single row, but remember that they will form a screen about 2–2.5m (6–8ft) high, so plant them in a position so that they will not shade the rest of the garden from the sun. Another word of warning: beware if you have a predisposition to gales in Fortes and Cromerty – they can be pretty windy for some people. It is a perennial plant that can just be left to grow year after year. Delicious grated, raw, in salads or cooked for about two or three minutes in boiling water.

CELERIAC: sown in the greenhouse in mid-spring and planted out in May. Again good raw in salads or cooked in a variety of ways. Can be stored all winter.

SALSIFY AND SCORZONERA: sown directly into the soil in mid-spring, these are similar to each other, both having long, thin roots, but salsify is white and scorzonera is black. Excellent as a starter with a vinaigrette sauce.

SWEDE: not really uncommon, but it seems to be becoming more so, perhaps because of people's memories of it in school dinners. A pity, because it is a superb vegetable that will store all winter.

Mashed with butter and black pepper, it's fit for a king.

Salad vegetables

CHICORY: there are two types – greenleaf (or red if it is the radicchio variety) and forcing chicory. Greenleaf chicory forms big hearts like lettuce, but can be harvested in autumn and stored for several weeks by hanging it in the shed. Forcing chicory is dug from November onwards, through the winter. Trim off the leaves to about 1cm ($^1/_2$in) from the top of the root, set the roots upright in a deep box or pot of compost or leaf mould, and store in a frost-free shed. Either cover with black polythene to exclude the light or cover the roots with a layer of compost. The 'chicons', which will grow on the top of the root, can be harvested about six weeks later. A really wonderful addition to winter salads.

ENDIVE: the summer varieties are just a coarse version of lettuce, but winter varieties can be a very sweet and useful substitute for lettuce in the winter. Geoff recommended sowing in late summer and, when the plant was about three months old, covering with a flowerpot with its drainage hole blocked to exclude light. This will blanch and soften the endive.

ROCKET: not to everybody's taste, but some people go crazy for it in winter or summer salads. It has a peppery taste and is sown from spring to mid-summer. I have found spring and autumn sowings the best, as it tends to go to seed quickly in summer.

MUSTARD AND CRESS: a useful crop which people seem to forget about after they leave primary school. Grown on damp blotting paper on the windowsill, or outside when the danger of frost has past. Nothing could be easier.

Leaf vegetables

CALABRESE: a useful brassica which delivers dense heads like broccoli early in the season. Harvest the main head first and allow the side shoots to develop.

CHINESE CABBAGE: sown in spring to mid-summer, a prolific salad vegetable with a dense white heart.

PAK CHOI: one of Geoff's favourites. Easy to grow and produces succulent leaves and stems that are excellent in salads and unbeatable as a stir-fry vegetable.

FLORENCE FENNEL: sown in late summer, it produces swollen stems with a delicate aniseed flavour. It will need to be covered with cloches for winter use. Braised in the oven it makes a very trendy dish with which to impress your friends at a dinner party.

Vegetable fruits

SQUASH: an underrated vegetable with a huge diversity of varieties, in all shapes, colours and sizes, so experiment to decide which varieties you like best. Squashes are grown just like marrows, but if you have too little room to grow them this way try growing them up a support. You will have to tie them in as they grow and support the fruit when it gets heavy, but it is well worth the effort. Geoff's favourites were 'Little Gem' and 'Jack Be Little'. Harvest in the autumn when the sun has ripened them and they will store for at least three months. Poke some holes in the skin to stop them exploding, pop them in the oven for twenty minutes, or the microwave for three, cut off the top, scoop out the seeds, knob of butter, sprinkle of black pepper, and you have the best starter you have ever tasted.

MULTIPLE SEEDING

Multiple seeding – sowing more than one seed to a module – is a technique developed for commercial growers, which Geoff adapted to fit the needs of ordinary gardeners.

Instead of sowing one seed per module, you sow several seeds, the number varying according to the crop. Multiple seeding is not suitable for long-rooted crops like some varieties of carrots, parsnips, etc., because they simply wind their roots round each other, but it will work with a large number of other plants. Sow the required number of seeds in each module and cover with a fine layer of silver sand or vermiculite. When they are ready, plant them outside and the plants simply push each other apart as they grow, with no thinning required.

At Barnsdale this method is used mainly for early crops that are to be planted out into deep beds, but there is no reason why multiple-seeded crops should not be grown all the year round, provided you have the greenhouse space. Geoff tried multiple seeding many different crops, but the ones he most favoured, and finally settled for, were:

ONIONS: sow six seeds per module in mid- to late January and plant out in March/April, preferably protected with a cloche. 'Hygro' is a good variety for this purpose, and it stores very well.

BEETROOT: sow two to three seeds per module, as each seed case already contains several seeds. If more than six seedlings emerge, remove the excess. Plant out in March/April.

LEEKS: sow them, in exactly the same way as onions, and then plant them in blocks, 30cm (12in) apart each way. Planted so close, and multiple seeded, they blanch each other, and the shorter and slightly narrower stems are easily compensated for by the much higher yield.

CARROTS: carrots can be multiple seeded, provided you use an early, stump-rooted variety such as 'Lola'. Sow six seeds to a module and plant out in March/April. Grown under a cloche in a deep bed they will give you an abundant crop of the sweetest carrots you have ever tasted.

TURNIPS: 'Purple Top Milan' was the only turnip Geoff would consider for multiple sowing. Grow in the same way as carrots.

RADISH AND SALAD ONIONS: multiple seeding is very good for an early sowing, but of doubtful value later as they are so easy to grow directly in the soil. Again, deal with them as you would carrots.

SPINACH: a very valuable crop if sown in January/February, two or three seeds per module, as it matures quickly, particularly if protected by a cloche. It will give you a welcome green vegetable before there is much else about.

Opposite: Geoff was never averse to growing flowers and vegetables together, even on his allotment.

146

I bless the day Geoff introduced me to multiple seeding: it has has given me a good supply of succulent vegetables very early every season. I plant them all in a deep bed, under one of Geoff's clever cloches (see page 82), and we toast him every time we eat them.

The Parterre Garden

Geoff was always anxious to build a herb garden. He said he wanted one because the herbs would disguise the taste of Lynda's cooking, but I have tasted Lynda's cooking and I can vouch for the fact that that was a wicked deception.

If the herb garden was going to be built at all the approach had to be an interesting and novel one for television. So Geoff chose what was perhaps the least novel of all his ideas — what the French call a parterre, which was novel in the sixteenth century. A parterre is simply a series of very small beds, set out in a formal design and sometimes bounded by box hedges, santolina or even miniature berberis. The beds are normally 1m (3ft) to 1.3m (4ft) wide which makes them easy to manage because they can be reached from either side without the need to tread on the soil. This makes the parterre ideal for people like me who have to face the fact that they are marginally past the full bloom of youth. In the event, Geoff decided to build a parterre that contained not only herbs, but vegetables and some flowers as well. He surounded the whole area with box (*Buxus sempervirens*), setting the plants about 15cm (6in) apart. Each bed was bounded by wood in this case, but any of the plants described above could be used. Brick paths gave a mellow finish to a delightful feature.

He kept the herbs down to six, in this case using chervil, dill marjoram, parsley, thyme and golden sage, which should be enough for most culinary needs and will certainly provide a very pleasing feature, although if herbs are your heart's desire you can obviously make the bed as big as you like.

The £2 Garden

As soon as Geoff became a gardening writer, and all the more so when he was later given the opportunity to present his ideas on television, gardening for him ceased to be just a vocation and a career. It became a mission — and he executed that mission with as much zeal and exuberance as he could muster.

He was particularly interested in introducing young people to gardening and showing them how it would give them lots of fun and, at the same time, good food for their families, without having to spend a

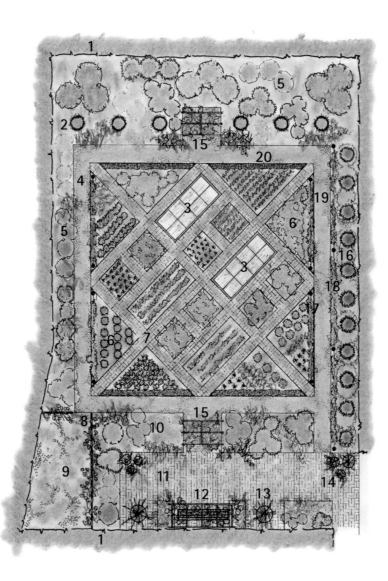

1   Hedge

2   Standard gooseberry

3   Cold frame

4   Grass path

5   Mixed border

6   Vegetables in deep beds

7   Brick paving

8   Trellis

9   Gravel storage area

10 Herb planting

11   Brick paving

12 Arbour

13 Pot

14 Pots

15 Arch with fan-trained apples

16 Soft fruit

17 Fan-trained apples

18 Step-over trained apples

19 Grass path

20 Box hedge

A well-maintained parterre is not only a delight to the eye but also a fruitful source of vegetables and flowers.

There is nothing so
satisfying as harvesting
a good crop of potatoes.

fortune. Gardening is one of the most convenient and most satisfying occupations there is, and one of the least expensive. After all, there is no subscription involved in joining the gardening club outside your back door, you will not have to travel miles to get to it and there will be no rounds of drinks to buy at the end of a day's sport. But people would argue with him that this is not the case. And it is true that you can spend serious money on seeds, plants, fertilizers, compost, seed trays, tools, cloches, etc. Not to mention all the little things that mount up into a substantial sum – string, labels, gloves, hoses, watering cans and a host of other incidental but necessary items. So for most young people trying to bring up a young family gardening appears to be just not feasible – and they don't do it.

So Geoff decided to show how gardening could be done inexpensively– and to show it to the Great British Public on television, and the idea for the £2 Garden was born. He would demonstrate how a family of three could move into a new house and build up a whole garden, from scratch, on a budget of no more than £2 a week. (Actually £104 per year, as it would not be possible to spread the expenditure evenly.)

First a few assumptions were made. It was assumed that a basic tool kit was available – a wedding present, perhaps. This consisted of a spade, a fork, a rake and a hoe, as well as a small lawn mower. The rest of the tools would have to be made. Geoff also assumed a 2.5 x 1.8m (8 x 6ft) greenhouse. In the programme he included a lawn and borders in his plan, and therefore in his budget, but the principle focus was on the vegetable garden, which is what I shall concentrate on here. Remember also that the programme was screened in 1984, so things were a bit cheaper then; but on the other hand people earn more today, so the principles still apply.

BODY AND SOIL

Geoff applied all his organic gardening principles to the £2 Garden, with the starting point always being the soil. So he recommended all the things I have described on pages 35-6, including, of course making compost so that organic matter could be continually added to the soil. But he was worried about spending money on a compost container. In fact he said in his book *The £2 Garden,* 'I had decided at the outset that my limited budget wouldn't allow me to buy one of those smart compost containers my wealthy brother uses.' I had begging letters for months after that! So he used an old plastic fertilizer bag. He simply cut some holes into it, about the size of a 10p piece, and filled it with compost material, tying the top when it was full.

When he made the compost he found he had another problem: he had more grass cuttings than weeds, which he needed to mix with the grass cuttings to give the bacteria some breathing space, so the grass cuttings settled into a slimy mess. His budget would not run to a bale of straw, which is what I use when I run out of other aerating material, so he cut old newspapers into 1cm ($\frac{1}{2}$in) strips and, just before he added his grass cuttings, he would soak the strips in liquid fertilizer; and this did the trick, not just aerating the compost, but activating it as well. He found it took quite a time to fill one bag, because decomposition starts straight away and the material settles quickly. Nevertheless after one season he found he had thirteen bags of good material, which he got for next to nothing.

He grew most of the vegetables in four deep beds (see page 139), about 3m (10ft) long and 1.25m (4ft) wide, because this gave him the opportunity to grow really intensively and thus get the most out of a small space. He did not grow maincrop potatoes, because he felt they would take up too much space and they were the one crop that would be as good and as cheap from the greengrocer. But he devoted one entire bed to a crop of earlies, grown under plastic in the way described on page 82. He did not spend any money on the plastic. This was in the days before the ubiquitous wheelie-bin, when the dustperson would obligingly leave several spare bags tucked in the handle of the dustbin; nowadays you can buy them. Cut them up, anchor them with soil and you can plant the tubers through holes cut in the plastic. Growing them like this saves earthing them up as well. All you do when you are ready to harvest is lift the plastic and you will find the tubers lying invitingly on the soil, just begging to be cooked.

Geoff did not grow runner beans on his deep beds either, because they do not lend themselves to that kind of cultivation. Instead he grew them beside the greenhouse, firstly because the young plants would benefit from the heat reflected from the glass and secondly because the mature crop would provide much-needed shade for the greenhouse in summer. Thus he saved another few vital pennies on shading material.

Many vegetables can be stored right through the winter, cutting the greengrocery bills in half.

CHOOSING VARIETIES

In the £2 Garden Geoff was particularly conscious of the need to keep the cost of seeds down. So he urged the £2 gardener not to do as he did, but to think very carefully about the choice of seeds, since this could save a great deal of money. For example, he advised avoiding many of the F1 hybrids. They are much more expensive than open-pollinated types and they are developed for commercial growers who need uniformity of size and ripening, which is just what the amateur gardener doesn't want, except perhaps with crops like tomatoes and sweet corn, for which early ripening is important.

Another way to reduce the seed bill is to choose only one variety for the whole season. Choosing more than one can be a way of spending money needlessly: for example, Geoff pointed out that one variety may be said to mature early, whilst another may be described as a good variety for storing, whereas in fact most early varieties will also store well and there is no necessity to buy two types.

Saving seed was another of Geoff's economies, although this is, of course, possible only after Year 1. For many plants this is not worth the space or the bother, but it is easy and useful to save seed from potatoes, runner beans, French beans, peas and broad beans. He also found that, in many cases, he did not use the whole packet of seed. If seeds are stored in their original foil, or simply in an envelope in a cool, dry place, they will do for the following year. In Geoff's first year he spent only £14 on seeds, and he estimated that this could be cut in half in Year 2.

GROWING UNDER CLOCHES

In addition to his amazing cloche (see page 82), which saved a great deal of money, Geoff suggested using plastic bottles with the bottom cut off, or jam jars, to protect individual plants. They both have the added advantage that they also protect against slugs. OK, they do not look so good, but if you are watching the pennies, who cares? For protecting individual rows he suggested 'finding' some stiff wire and bending it into hoops to support a narrow length of clear polythene to make a smaller version of his miracle cloche.

THE DREADED GREENHOUSE

Geoff agonized over the inclusion of the greenhouse, since a greenhouse is probably the most expensive piece of garden equipment to run and would eat deeply into his budget. He received a lot of letters from viewers saying that his thinking was cock-eyed and that he ought to be removed immediately to a house of correction. But he wrote polite letters to them and did it anyway. His justification for having one was that, since growing in a greenhouse is more expensive than growing outside, it would give him an extra challenge – and he was never one to turn his back on a challenge – and add interest to the programme.

COMPOST

Compost is one of the heaviest greenhouse expenses, so Geoff decided to mix his own. Now at the time he made this programme he had not yet realized the importance of preserving peat, so his recommendation was for a peat-based compost. If I mention what it was I risk a bolt of lightning again, because Geoff would certainly not have recommended that now. He would be suggesting a coir seed or potting compost instead (see page 64).

SEED CONTAINERS

When you consider the price of seed trays, pots and modules today it will be obvious that Geoff's budget could never have stood the racket, but in our throwaway world there are dozens of suitable containers that can be recycled – which will save you money and release a little more space in a landfill site somewhere.

For sowing he found that the polystyrene trays that are used to contain meat and fish from supermarkets are ideal. You just need to punch a few small holes in the bottom for drainage. These trays are, however, a bit too shallow for seedlings which have to be grown on, so Geoff racked his brains for the ideal container for this purpose and came up with – wait for it – the Chinese takeaway trays that contain your chop suey and fried rice. To have enough I think you would have to ask your friends to save them for you as well, or else you would have to eat so many takeaways that you would have no time for the garden. He also suggested a visit to an electrical goods shop, because their appliances are delivered in polystyrene packing, much of which makes excellent trays, although you may have to cut them up with a serrated-edged knife.

For pots he suggested plastic coffee cups, waxed milk containers, tins with their tops cut away cleanly so as not to leave jagged edges – in fact there are dozens of throwaway items that would do. He made module trays from old cardboard egg trays, with the bottom sliced off, so that the compost in them would be in contact with the capillary matting on the staging (although it was not in fact capillary matting, as we shall see). He used these mainly to sow multiple-seeded crops and, when they were ready to plant out, simply cut up the tray and planted the whole thing, so as to cause minimum root disturbance; the tray would just rot away as the plants grew.

Cabbage 'Durham Early'.

Potato 'Nadine'.

Cauliflower 'Fleurly'.

CONSERVING HEAT

In his greenhouse Geoff clearly could not afford heat, which would have run away with his entire budget in the first couple of months. So he decided to try to grow from January, right through the year, without any artificial heat at all – quite a task. His first move was to insulate the bottom layers of glass, underneath the staging, since no light was needed there. This meant another trip to the electrical shop to lean politely on the proprietor for more polystyrene. This time he was looking for blocks of material, which would line the greenhouse, held in place with nylon string.

This took good care of the bottom, but the most important part to insulate is the area above the staging. Although it is possible to line the roof with a sheet of polythene to provide a form of double glazing, Geoff did not like this, as it reduces light levels substantially, so he adapted a method that commercial growers use successfully, the thermal screen. In commercial houses this is a sheet of clear insulating material that slides automatically over the seedlings at pre-set times, but the amateur gardener obviously could not afford that. So Geoff bought a sheet of clear polythene and fixed it to battens at 60cm (2ft) intervals, and then tied some strong nylon line along the sides of the house, just below the eaves. He fixed the polythene at the back of the house, with the battens spanning it and resting on the two strings. At night he could pull the polythene towards the door to cover the plants, then in the morning his first job was to push the polythene screen back again. Geoff found doing this a bit fiddly and he confessed to using language that would have been unacceptable to the neighbours if he had had any. But it protected his precious vegetable seeds very well, so his advice was to do it but to try to moderate your language.

WATERING

By the time Geoff got to think about how he was going to water in his greenhouse his budget was in serious disarray and he could not afford a watering can. Watering the pots was easy because he used either a bucket and an old milk bottle or he borrowed the teapot from the house. But the problem of watering the seeds, which need a fine spray, taxed him a little more. He came up with the idea of using a plastic cooking-oil bottle with some pinholes in the lid, and each morning he could be seen happily squeezing and refilling from his old bucket – a contented man.

Geoff wanted to use capillary matting on his staging (see page 65), but he decided that this was an expense too far. So he took a trip to the local carpet store, found the manager, pleaded abject poverty and was able to scrounge some offcuts of felt carpet underlay, which did the trick perfectly, used in the same way as capillary matting. He cut the matting so as to

create a tongue at the end that could be immersed in a bucket of water, thus keeping the underlay wet all the time, and he had the perfect watering system – for nothing.

Growing on deep beds is a very economical way to use a small plot of land.

GROWING BAGS

Tomatoes, cucumbers, melons and aubergines were all to be grown in growing bags, after the staging had been dismantled in May/June, when the other plants had been planted out. Again Geoff decided that he would make his own. He filled a plastic fertilizer bag with compost, stapled the ends together with an ordinary office stapler and cut three holes in the bag to provide the growing space. In fact, even after the £2 Garden he never bought another growing bag again. In later years he filled them with leaf mould.

There were many other small economies that Geoff made: 'whalehide' pots for peppers and aubergines, made by using one bought real pot as a template to make others from polythene cut from a fertilizer bag; a plant 'solarium' for the windowsill, made from an orange box covered in foil to reflect light; a strawberry pot made from a plastic barrel with holes cut in the sides for planting; and even a hanging basket made from old roof laths joined with nylon string.

At the end of the experiment he had incurred costs of £95. This amount included £11 of capital costs that would not be incurred in future years. The amount he had saved on vegetables that would otherwise have to have been bought was £140. In all he made a profit of £45. Not tycoon money, but enough, he hoped, to convince a lot of young people that gardening on a £2-a-week budget can and should be done.

Creating special environments

A BOISTEROUSLY BUCOLIC BACKGROUND

I cannot tell you how many evenings I spent listening to Geoff railing against the way farmers tear up their hedges, planners allow green-belt land to get swallowed up by building, motorways spread concrete and pollution across once pleasant acres, airports ruin quiet communities with noise and so on. OK, he did not want to go back to transportation for sheep stealing, or sending little boys up chimneys, or smallpox or consumption. He much appreciated many of the benefits that modern life brings. After all, without television, who would have heard of Geoff Hamilton? And he was enough of a realist to know that progress cannot be halted. But he felt strongly that in some ways the developments of the modern world were reducing the quality of our lives dramatically. He felt that, apart from the negative effects of the despoliation of the countryside, we were suffering from our lives becoming too complex. He read descriptions of the old rural way of life – *Historia Plantarum* by John Ray, *Rural Rides* by William Cobbett, *Larkrise to Candleford* by Flora Thompson and many others – and they left him with a conviction that we had lost a valuable part of life by destroying its diversity.

So he decided to create gardens of different environments, to try to show how the garden could become a place of diversity, a collection of such environments, each springing its own surprise on an unsuspecting guest.

Alpines and the Scree Gardens

A scree garden is really an environment for alpine plants, which in natural conditions would be found growing on rocky hills and mountainsides, usually sheltering in cracks and crevices in the rock. Geoff didn't believe in creating artificially 'natural' environments, like the piles of rock posing as mountains that one sometimes sees in suburban back gardens, because they tend to look exactly what they are – artificial. He felt it was better to own up to the fact that a glacier had not recently transformed your garden and to make it honestly artificial.

He built two Scree Gardens at Barnsdale, one rectangular and one circular, both formal, and both very beautiful throughout the year. The circular bed was edged with paving bricks, each brick pointing exactly into the centre, and subsequently pointed with mortar. The rectangular bed was

Geoff's Scree Gardens are filled with delicate, brightly flowering scented plants.

edged with three courses of bricks so that the bed could be raised, because it was in a position where the drainage was not so good. Then he filled both beds with a free-draining, gritty compost, as alpines can stand any amount of cold, but they cannot tolerate wet, so it is important to ensure that the drainage is good. He also added some stepping stones to the flat bed, which not only made an attractive feature but allowed access to all the plants.

Finally Geoff planted both beds with miniature bulbs such as narcissus and muscari to give some very early spring colour, and with alpine plants chosen to provide something to be in flower all year. These included *Saxifraga* species – delightful little plants which form small cushions of pink to white flowers, house leeks or sempervivum, and sedums, which both have succulent leaves and grow in a wide variety of forms; *Pulsatilla* species, which have nodding, bell-shaped flowers ranging from dark red to purple; phlox – a plant normally associated with the cottage garden border, but the alpine varieties are compact and delicate, with flowers of pink through to purple; and, amongst the most colourful of the alpines, the *Cistus* species or rock roses, which have pink or white flowers, often spectacularly

MAKING A HYPERTUFA TROUGH

marked with yellow and red spots. To add height he used genuine dwarf evergreens such as *Juniperus communis* and dwarf cytisus varieties like *Cytisus x beanii*, one of the smaller brooms.

Geoff's Scree Gardens looked so realistically like the Austrian Tyrol that I expected him to appear in lederhosen, slapping his knees and singing 'oompah' songs. His enthusiasm for them was so great that I certainly would not have put it past him.

There are innumerable varieties of alpines to choose from, but when making your choice you should take care to ensure that they are tolerant of wet conditions. If not, you will certainly lose them in a wet winter. The most vulnerable are usually the ones with woolly grey leaves.

The only way to grow alpines that are not rain-hardy is to grow them in a greenhouse. The house should be as airy as possible and given maximum ventilation all winter, with shading in summer if the sun is strong. This was another environment that Geoff created and his alpine house was a blaze of colour in late winter and right through the summer. But he recognized that there would not be many people who could afford to devote a whole greenhouse to alpines, so he designed a small portable cover for alpines in outside beds. It consisted of a wooden frame, covered with rigid PVC, which slotted into pipes at the corner of a raised bed, so that it would provide protection in the winter and could be removed in spring. Alternatively it is possible to protect individual plants with a small sheet of glass, clipped on to and supported by wire legs.

Geoff also recommended growing alpines in stone troughs, if you have insufficient room for a scree garden. What is more, he came up with a very nifty idea for making your own out of 'hypertufa', if you cannot afford to buy.

Take two square or rectangular cardboard boxes, one about 5cm (2in) smaller all round than the other. Make the hypertufa from one part cement and two of sieved coconut fibre compost mixed with one part sharp sand. Put a 2.5cm (1in) layer of hypertufa, mixed fairly wet, into the bottom of the larger box and lay a piece of chicken wire on top to provide reinforcement. Put a further 2.5cm (1in) layer of hypertufa on top of the netting. Cut four 5cm (2in) pieces of broom handle and push them through the netting, to make drainage holes and provide a base for the smaller box to sit on. Cut some more reinforcing wire and make it into a rectangle 2.5cm (1in) wider than the smaller box, so that it will sit between the two boxes. Then fill the space between the two boxes with hypertufa .and push it down with a stick, making sure there are no air spaces. As the wet mixture will soften the box fill the inside box with bricks and push some paving stones or wood against the outer box to support it while it dries. Next day remove the wet cardboard and round off the rough edges with a knife.

The Man-made Rock Garden

The epoch of the man-made rock garden was the time when I began to entertain doubts about Geoff's psychological well-being. It happened like this.

During his contacts with his colleagues in horticulture, and particularly those who shared his radical views about the preservation of the environment, Geoff began to learn of the wanton destruction of limestone pavements, particularly in North Yorkshire — majestic outcrops of rock which house hundreds of different varieties of rock plants. So, ever the action man, he decided to go up to see for himself. And who better to go with than his very dear friend Roy Lancaster — certainly one of the foremost plantsmen in Europe, who has an intimate knowledge of this particular environment and its wildlife.

They spent a morning scrambling over rough terrain, with Roy pointing out plants Geoff had never seen — many of them hanging on tenaciously to life in what seemed to be the most hostile of conditions. Geoff became more and more excited and his imagination began to work on how he could reproduce what he was seeing at Barnsdale, to show others how it could be done.

And then he had an almost exact replay of the experience he had had when he looked at peat bogs in Ireland. Just over the brow of the hill was a huge bulldozer and a mechanical shovel, tearing the pavement apart and loading it on to trucks for delivery to unsuspecting and innocent gardeners to make garden rockeries in suburbia. With the stone went all the plant life and what was left was a bombsite that would take literally centuries to regenerate. Geoff was horrified and Roy was angry, and they left feeling determined to do what they could to stop it.

A hypertufa trough planted with alpines.

Geoff's view was that he should try to dissuade gardeners from using stone at all. But what a tough assignment. Nobody would stop unless they had an alternative — so Geoff decided it was his job to provide them with one. I was used to Geoff's eccentricities, and I knew most artists go through a 'loony' period, but at this point I began to think his sanity was departing him.

From then on he could be seen, grim-faced and jutting-jawed as his determination took hold, digging small holes in the ground, lining

them with plastic sheet and filling them with a coir, sand and concrete mix to which he had added a cement dye to make it look more like stone. When his 'stones' were set he would dig them out and line them up in gradations of colour, the better to make his judgment about which suited him best.

Now to me they looked like concrete lumps, just like those you could find on any building site – certainly not the kind of thing anybody would want in their garden. When I tackled Geoff about this he gave me one of his benign grins and said, 'See what you think when I've got them laid and planted up.' Well, I left him that day with a strong feeling that the strain of his job was getting to be too much, and racking my brains for the name of a good psychiatrist.

But a couple of weeks later I went back, to find that he had perfected the colour and shapes he wanted, built them into a rockery and planted them up with the kind of alpines mentioned earlier. It looked stunning, and I found myself, once again, having to admit that perhaps he was right and having to cancel the appointment with the psychiatrist.

Geoff demonstrated this method on *Gardeners' World* and took the opportunity to draw attention to the plight of the limestone pavements. He also wrote a good deal about it in an effort to highlight the importance

Geoff looks with pride on his artificial stone, which may help to preserve limestone pavements.

of preserving this imposing but delicate environment. When the wildflower conservation charity Plantlife began a campaign to protect limestone pavements, they asked Geoff to front it, which he did and he worked hard to publicize the cause.

The Water Garden

When Geoff and I were about four years old we decided, one hot summer, that what we needed in our garden was a swimming pool. So, disregarding the vegetables that were planted in neat rows in our father's 'Dig for Victory' campaign, we dug a large hole in the soil, filled it with water from the hose and jumped in. We were a little disappointed that the water drained away so quickly and that we had created so much mud, but we found that as long as we kept the hose running at full bore we could have a good paddle. I should perhaps add that our parents had nipped next door at the time. Expecting praise for our enterprise on their return, we were surprised to find that Dad did not seem to see it that way. Two muddy little boys were dragged off to the bathroom and put to bed with no supper – an injustice that still smoulders inside.

I cannot be sure, but I suspect that it was this experience which started Geoff's appetite for water gardens. All men are boys at heart and playing with water is certainly great fun.

Geoff loved water features, because they invite wildlife into the garden and provide habitats for an exciting range of plants, and also because they bring a sense of harmony and tranquillity into the garden. A water feature can be simply a calm, still pool or, with the help of an electric pump, you can have tumbling waterfalls, rippling streams or gushing fountains.

The Water Garden at Barnsdale started life as a pond with a surrounding bog garden. First Geoff dug and lined the pond in the way described below, in this case in a circular shape, although you can use any shape that takes your fancy, of course. He then dug a further, shallower hole around the pond to form the bog garden. This he filled completely with soil, setting it at a level that would ensure that the water from the pond fed the bog garden. At the shallow part of the pond he made a pleasing 'beach', using large pebbles, to give wading birds easy access to the pond.

But after he had dug the hole for the pond and bog garden, we could almost see his mind working on some slight dissatisfaction.

Sure enough, the following day, whilst having a break for coffee with Lynda, he said, 'I think what that pond needs is a stream to feed it.'

So, leaving his coffee, it was into the tool shed for his trusty spade, a march to his bog garden and Geoff began work. First he marked out where

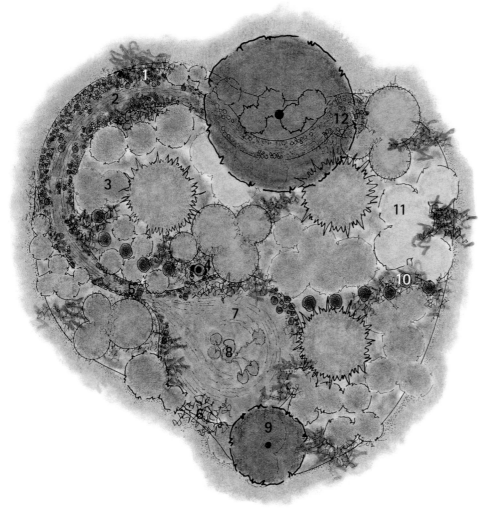

1 Boulder and cobbles

2 Stream

3 Bog area for moisture-loving plants

4 Focal point

5 Timber waterfall

6 Marginal planting

7 Pond [as described in text]

8 Water lilies

9 Tree planting

10 Timber stepping stones

11 Architectural planting

12 Pump outlet

Left: Geoff hid little statues in unusual places to surprise his friends.

Right: The magnificent structural plants in the bog garden give an almost prehistoric effect.

Top: Trollius europaeus,
a gloriously sunny bog
plant.

Above: The marsh
marigold, *Caltha*
palustris.

the stream was to go and then he dug it out to a depth of about 15cm (6in). It is a mistake to dig too deep a channel because if it is full it will deprive the pond of too much water and if it is not full you will see a large expanse of butyl liner at the sides. He took care to ensure that the stream sloped down from the pond slightly, so that the water would remain in the stream even when the pump that he was going to install was switched off. Next he laid butyl liner on the bottom and sides of the stream, tucking and folding it to make it as neat as possible, and leaving the excess material overhanging the edge. This he covered with soil and laid a strip of turf on top to finish it off. Finally he laid rocks and pebbles in the bottom of the channel so that the water would respond with a gentle rippling sound and the stream would look more natural and pleasing.

He installed an electric pump to take water from the pond to the top of the stream and he produced, with the flick of a switch, a genuine stream, which gurgled and bubbled down to the pond, just like a natural stream.

Then came the time for the planting, a job that Geoff relished, firstly because it gave him another opportunity to set his imagination to work and secondly because it enabled him to get wet and muddy and return to his childhood without fear of losing his supper. At the shallow edges of the pond he used marginal plants such as the marsh marigold, *Caltha palustris*, the water forget-me-not, *Myosotis scorpioides*, and the Arum lily, *Zantedeschia aethiopica*. As the water deepened he planted plants that required different planting depths. *Iris laevigata* was one of Geoff's great favourites, planted in about 15cm (6in) of water, and he also used the bogbean, *Menyanthes trifoliata*, which grows in about 23cm (9in) of water. In the deep water, he planted the larger water lilies, as well as the water hawthorn, *Aponogeton distachyos*, in baskets with pebbles on the surface to keep the soil in place.

He also added some floating plants, just throwing them in, but he avoided things like fairy moss and duckweed because they quickly cover the surface and are difficult to get rid of. He also added oxygenating weed, which is really just another floating plant, because it helps to keep the water clear of algae; it is also an essential if the pond is to be stocked with fish. Geoff recommended *Lagarosiphon major* syn. *Elodea crispa* as an oxygenating weed because it is easy to control, although even it has to be removed from time to time. He was always careful to point out that if the pond is to be cleared of floating weed it should be left on the edge of the pond for a day or so, to enable the wildlife that will be sheltering in it to return to the pond.

Planting the bog garden was a chance for Geoff to indulge his undoubted taste for high drama, because there are some wonderful bog plants that will give an exotic, almost tropical effect. *Gunnera manicata* for example, grows enormous leaves and can reach heights of 3m (10ft) if it has an unlimited root run. The giant Chinese rhubarb, *Rheum palmatum*, is a similar plant, more suitable for the smaller garden, as it does not reach the same height. Then there are the *Trollius* species, which can be guaranteed to give a good show of yellow and orange flowers over a long period; all the irises, which are quite happy in wet soil; *Astilbe* x *arendsii*, with fern-like foliage, which will flower for a long period; and another great favourite with Geoff, the umbrella plant, *Darmera peltata*, which is a superb architectural plant, growing to 90cm (36in), with rounded leaves topped by flat heads of pink flowers.

The pond, bog garden and stream seemed to become one of Geoff's great prides. He was never a boastful man — far from it: I would have to drag from him information about accolades he had received as though it was an MI5 interrogation — but he delighted in showing his gardening achievements to his friends. And Lynda and I, who were probably his best friends, were repeatedly marched off for 'admiring time' at his bog garden, stream and pond. We, of course, nodded and applauded and dutifully provided the approbation this part of the garden deserved.

The Mediterranean Garden

Lynda is a fluent French linguist and she would often drag Geoff from his beloved Barnsdale across to France for a break. He would go kicking and screaming but inevitably they would end up looking at gardens and he became enchanted with many of the small gardens in the south that are a riot of colour and form. There is hardly a single French house without its containers of pelargoniums and busy lizzies, and at the back of the house, however small, a wonderland of alliums, cistus, salvias, osteospermum, artemisia, thymes, etc., not to mention garlic, globe artichokes, tomatoes, grapes, olives, figs and all the other fruit and vegetables one associates with the French way of life.

Even in the frost the plants on the little patio look miraculously. beautiful.

Taken with a fit of Francophilia after one of his trips, Geoff decided to try to emulate the bright, colourful borders that he and Lynda had admired in France in a hot, south-facing area in the courtyard garden that surrounds the house at Barnsdale. He began, as always, by conditioning his soil. Mediterranean plants thrive on very free-draining, dry soils that bask in sunshine for most of the day. Although Geoff's site was right the soil was too heavy and water-retentive. So, once again, he called for the spade, which now seemed to have become an appendage to him, and got to work, incorporating loads of grit, to transform the soil into a light and friable condition.

Next came some exciting trips to specialist nurseries to find the plants he needed. He had designed mainly round beds, so he decided against very tall specimens, preferring to go for a maximum height of about 90cm (36in), to ensure that the view across the garden would not be obstructed. The plants he chose for the centre of the round borders were *Yucca recurvifolia*, with blue-green, tapered and pointed leaves and creamy flowers in summer; *Salvia nubicola*, with pale green leaves and pale yellow flowers in late summer and autumn; and *Artemisia lactiflora* Guizhou Group, a plant which delivers a three-fold gift of red-brown stems, cream flowers and striking seed heads; as well as *Cistus* x *aguilarii* 'Maculatus', a striking plant with narrow, grey-green leaves and white flowers with crimson blotches.

He surrounded these larger plants with plants of medium height, such as *Daphne tangutica*, a real bonus, with dark green leaves, cream-purple, heavily scented, flowers in spring followed by red berries; and *Parahebe perfoliata*, which has grey-green leaves and violet flowers in late summer. Also with grey-green leaves but this time with lemon yellow, scented, pea-like flowers, *Coronilla valentina* subsp. *glauca* 'Citrina' really appealed to Geoff, as did *Digitalis parviflora*, which has dark, brown-tinged leaves and tiny brown flowers in summer.

He also went for a number of species that were suitable for drying, so that the house would have summer brightness all through the dark days of winter: *Lavandula stoechas*, which has dark purple, tufted flowers in summer; *Pennisetum villosum*, which is a narrow-leaved grass with fluffy cream flower

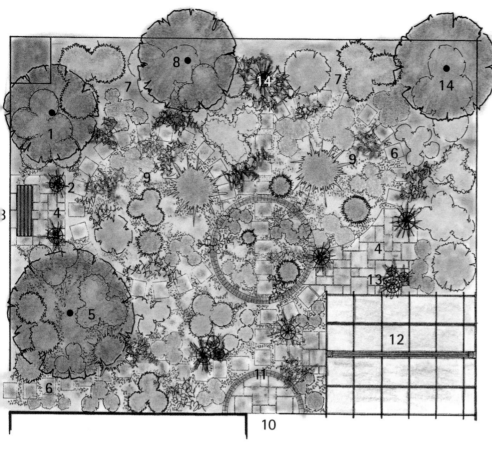

1 *Malus*

2 Pot

3 Seat

4 Random paving

5 *Prunus*

6 Stepping stones

7 Shade-loving plants

8 *Prunus*

9 Mediterranean planting in gravel

10 Gate

11 Blue brick edge

12 Timber glasshouse

13 Pots

14 *Acer*

15 Large pot

Part of the Mediterranean Garden, shortly after it was made, beginning to take shape.

heads in late summer; and *Eryngium* x *tripartitum*, which has dark green, toothed leaves and grey-blue flower heads in late summer.

The front of the borders was filled with plants like *Onosma albo-roseum* with grey-green leaves and pale pink flowers in summer; *Dianthus deltoides* with delicate red-pink flowers from early summer to autumn; and a plant that gives really good value, *Erigeron speciosus* 'Felicity', which has pink and white daisy-like flowers from late spring right through to autumn.

All in all, the Mediterranean Garden, which Geoff had skilfully planned to set his little courtyard alight with colour from early spring to late autumn, had a climate of sunshine that would have done justice to any Frenchman.

The Reclaim Garden

The inspiration for the Reclaim Garden can be put down partly to Geoff's environmental mission and partly to his abiding passion for junk. Ever since we were small, Geoff and I would prowl round junk shops, demolition yards and, dare I admit it, rubbish dumps, in search of anything useful or interesting that we could get for nothing or for a few pence. Geoff's workshop at Barnsdale still has shelves full of tins, Bakelite containers, old tools and various peculiar racks for implements lost long ago.

When Geoff got to Barnsdale he would often take himself off to one of the local demolition yards, usually an incredibly fruitful source of good junk. By now he was looking for the glittering prizes that you can still find if you look hard enough – Victorian edging tiles, chimney pots, old terracotta flower pots and other containers, and ancient wooden beams, which could all be used to make something attractive for the garden.

Some time before the Reclaim Garden was designed Geoff had advertised for a young landscape gardener. He wanted somebody who could both take some of the strain out of his job for him and be keen enough to learn how to design and build gardens to the very high standards that he achieved himself. He was amazed to receive an application from Adam Frost, the son of Martin Frost, who had worked with Geoff in his original landscaping business in Hertfordshire in the 1960s. Geoff had a great respect for Martin, a skilled and conscientious worker who helped him out of many a scrape and a potentially missed deadline. His immediate thought was that if Adam was as good as his dad, he was the man for the job. So he invited Adam up for interview and as much, I believe, from stirrings of old loyalties as from respect for Adam's skills – Adam had already been well trained, on two horticultural courses, so he was by no means a greenhorn – he offered him the job. The relationship turned out to be a dream ticket, and Geoff sent Adam off to Capel Manor to do a further course with David Stevens.

Adam came up with the proposal for the Reclaim Garden when Geoff asked him to kick a few ideas about for a new feature that they could include on *Gardeners' World*. Adam was greatly influenced by Geoff's concern for the environment and, after kicking a few ideas around, came up with a vision of a garden that was constructed entirely from reclaimed materials. Adam drew a rough sketch for the design and Geoff was so taken with it that he asked him to prepare a full design. When he saw this he suggested that it would be a good subject for their exhibit at the NEC *Gardeners' World Live* Exhibition and, demonstrating his faith in Adam's work, he simply said, 'I'll leave it all to you, boy.' Mind you, nothing would stop

When this imaginative sculpture was first made it had a sword in its hand, but Geoff, a peaceful man, substituted a hoe.

Geoff going with Adam to trawl demolition yards for materials, and they came back with some real treasures. All the materials were taken to the NEC to build the exhibition garden, but after the exhibition it was disassembled and rebuilt at Barnsdale, as a part of the weekly *Gardeners' World* programme.

The garden itself was small, as befitted an exhibition garden, and was bounded by elegant Victorian railings at the front and a close-boarded fence, made from old floor boarding, on the other sides. On entering one was faced by a small, circular lawn, with a simple bench to one side, made from a roof beam from an old demolished house.

At the other side of the lawn was a most unusual and attractive water feature made by Christian Funnel of Hove, a sculptor in metal who specializes in garden features. It was a small fountain made from an old copper water cistern, cunningly cut into the shape of a rose. The water chuckled down the 'petals', filling the air with the gentle sound of falling rain.

The most dramatic feature was undoubtedly the pergola, which took one through to the next part of the garden. It was made from reclaimed oak timbers, all jointed with pegs and dowels, with gently curving corner-braces. Clothed with roses, honeysuckle and clematis, it gave the height required in a small, intimate garden. The paths through the pergola were made from old York stone, perhaps the finest paving material to be found, and they were interspersed with reclaimed cobbles.

In the second 'room' the visitor was greeted by a delightful, humorous sculpture made from old garden machinery parts by Peter Cockburn of Rutland Garden and Machine Services in Oakham. It started life as a soldier, with a sword, but Geoff would not have anything that smacked of the arms trade on his patch, so he got the sculptor to remove the sword and replace it with a hoe.

The rest of this part of the garden was devoted to deep beds, edged with reclaimed railway sleepers, to grow vegetables and herbs for the table. Some old chimney pots were filled with tumbling tomatoes, nasturtiums and other colourful plants, and climbers of all kinds clambered up the fences, giving a verdant picture all round the garden, which was filled with a sense of antiquity and calm.

The stand was a roaring success at the NEC, winning not only an RHS Silver Gilt medal but also the BBC Award of Excellence for the Best Designed Garden. Adam (who did not know Geoff as well as I did, or he would have forecast this) was surprised when Geoff put his arm round his shoulders and said, 'You've done us proud, boy – that was a wonderful design,' and thrust £1000 into his hand. He really was some man!

The magical rose
fountain made from an
old water cistern.

1 Sculpture
2 Perennial and herb
planting
3 Pergola planted with
white roses
4 Raised vegetable beds
5 Box hedge (*Buxus
sempervirens*)
6 Chimney pots
7 Lawn
8 Sleeper retainer
9 Shrub and herbaceous
planting
10 Ornamental compost
bins
11 Cobbles
12 Water feature
13 Iron railings
14 York paving with cobble
inset
15 Clipped yew (*Taxus
baccatus*)
16 Timber bench
17 Pots

Geoff's private paradise

THE HISTORICAL SETTING

The history of gardens had always held a deep fascination for Geoff and he read a great deal about it, starting from the eighth century, when the Arabs brought their love and reverence for plants and gardens to Europe, during their conquest of Spain. He knew from his reading that all early civilizations shared this reverence and a great deal of pagan religion is based on the worship and thus the preservation of plants and animals, and the things that provide life – sun, rain and soil. He also knew, of course, that life in ancient times was little more than a constant search for food, shelter and warmth and for the vast majority of people there was no time for the luxury of lounging about in exotic gardens. For the poor, and the greatest proportion of people were poor, plants and animals were held in high regard because they provided food, building materials, fuel, clothing and bedding – almost all the necessities for the sustenance of life. Even the animals were housed inside their simple houses, not only to protect them from cold and predators but also to provide the earliest form of central heating.

This simple dependence on plants and animals continued right up to the Industrial Revolution in the late eighteenth century, when everything changed. Geoff felt that this was the point at which the decline of mankind began, with the pursuit of profit at the expense of the quality of life. I have to say that I did not entirely agree with this point of view, and this gave rise to yet more robust discussion over pints of Ruddles ale. I lamely argued industry's case – that our ability to deal with population growth, disease, housing, education and good food are all benefits arising from our industrial base and without it we would be a Third World country. But he certainly had a point. It was undeniable that hard-working conditions, Britain's sometime cruelty during the establishment of an empire, and the stress and poverty involved with working for barbarous masters interested only in profit all intensified after the establishment of an industrial base in Britain.

Well, our arguments would go on long into the night, but one thing we were both agreed upon: that the hurly-burly of modern life, the fourteen-hour days, the lack of job security and the seemingly endless demand for material things all have such a negative effect on the human spirit that you are much less likely to survive if you have not got a place of peace and tranquillity to retire to, marshal your thoughts and gird up your loins for

Opposite: The perennial border in the Town Garden was a subtle blend of colour and foliage, and alive with the gentle hum of insects.

the next assault. Showing people how to achieve that was Geoff's life's work and his abiding passion.

Geoff loved not only his own garden but all gardens and he had a burning desire to communicate this love to others, so that they too could share in the joys, both aesthetic and physical, of working to create a harmonious and radiant environment. He seriously worried about people forced by their circumstances to live in unpleasant high-rise blocks or noisy inner city developments (not to mention cardboard boxes). He knew from his own experience (because life had not always been 'easy street' for Geoff) the therapeutic value of building, maintaining and just contemplating an environment that you had created yourself, that was intensely beautiful and that aroused a little of the primeval longing for communion with nature.

He also knew that many people shied away from developing their own piece of precious land into anything other than a rectangular lawn with a straight border all round. This was usually because they viewed designing a beautiful garden as hard and unrewarding work, or they felt it would take up too much of their time, or because they lacked confidence in their own abilities to produce the exquisite results that Geoff demonstrated weekly on their television sets. So in the *Paradise Gardens* television programme he set out to show that it could be done – that all but the most seriously deprived could build their own private paradise, be it an estate in Edinburgh, an allotment in Aldershot or a windowbox in Willesden.

THE DESIGN

Geoff always counselled against getting too hung up on garden design. This was particularly true of his concept of a paradise garden, because it is essentially an intimate and heartfelt expression of the individuality of the gardener. He believed it was good to think about what you wanted, measure it carefully and draw it up on a piece of paper, but he did not think that any gardener should cherish the hope that they would get it all right the first time and that no more changes would be needed. Gardens evolve and change, as mistakes are made and then rectified, as plants outgrow their space and have to be moved or reduced in size, as new ideas come along and something has to give way for them – so you should regard the garden as an ever-changing thing, a living sculpture, that you can work on and improve as the years go by and as new thoughts occur to you. Geoff was a master at this, which is why he usually overplanted vastly to give dramatic effect and, as plants grew, thinned, pruned and shifted until he had the effect he was after. He also used to say to me that a good gardener is one who knows when to throw a plant away. I know he was right, but I

have to confess that I find that very difficult and I squirrel away plants in unlikely, odd corners of my garden, and as a result it now looks an incongruous jumble of afterthoughts.

Both the television programme and the book on *Paradise Gardens* were based on two gardens that Geoff designed, together with Adam Frost, his inspirational young colleague – one a town garden and the other a country garden. He also demonstrated additional ideas in other parts of Barnsdale, because they did not fit easily into the two designs. But Geoff was very, very keen to point out to his viewers and his readers that they should not slavishly follow his plans: their garden was their garden and not his, and they should stamp their own personality and aspirations on it. He also showed them the gardens of lots of other inventive people – ordinary people who had done extraordinary things with their gardens – to demonstrate other ways how, with a little thought and a lot of patience, it was possible to build a haven of seclusion and peace to provide a soothing refuge from a bustling world.

The mass of planting in this border mellows and softens the wall behind.

The Town Garden

The design for the Town Garden was centred around four boundary walls built in brick. Walled gardens are a wonderful source of shelter and warmth. I used to have one myself, attached to a Victorian house I lived in as a farm manager, and I can vouch for the fact that walls are a tremendous asset. But when Geoff was building the walls for the Town Garden they quickly began to take on the look of a giant warehouse. I had the temerity to mention this to Geoff, who just smiled at me and said, not for the first time, 'See what you think when it's finished'. Even he, though, admitted to some misgivings at first, when the walls were completed and he stood on the bare soil in the middle. He said he felt like a life-sentence prisoner in the exercise yard – lots of privacy, but no escape. Although the bricks were a mellow red it was clear that the stark squareness of the plot had to be relieved.

Geoff decided to do so with really intensive planting, which would soften the brick and lead the eye to a brilliant tapestry of colour and form. He also planned to erect an hexagonal conservatory against one wall and a small gazebo against another. With the walls clothed in climbers, a few trees, a small stream and pond and a beautifully shaped patio, he was confident that the design would work.

THE CONSERVATORY

The conservatory was, of course, a huge extravagance, but Geoff argued that it was a terrific investment, which would provide a leafy, secluded haven as well as adding another room to the house. One of the major advantages he saw was that a conservatory provides a refuge for the winter. Although it is easy to find a leafy hideaway during the summer, in winter a garden has a tendency to be cold and damp and bare; but with a conservatory you have your own haven with a sub-tropical climate in the next room. He went for a big structure, which at first sight, on the bare soil, looked very dominant. But Geoff felt that once it was filled with plants and surrounded by borders this effect would fade. When the garden was finished I was forced to admit that, despite my protestations, he was right again.

As with his own conservatory (described on page 88), he went for a wooden structure, because this enabled him to paint it a dark leaf green, which helped it to blend well into the background. He was not wedded to wood, which is expensive and needs constant maintenance, but for this garden, which he wanted to be a classic one, he felt the need to avoid plastic or aluminium, although either would be perfect in some situations.

The path from the conservatory to the front gate was straight. Geoff

1 Fern planting

2 Conservatory

3 Patio

4 Brick edge

5 Table and chairs

6 Gazebo

7 Lion's head fountain

8 Wall

9 Rill

10 Pool

11 *Acer palmatum*

12 Stepping-stone path

13 Irises planted in pots

14 Planting

15 Bog planting

This striking gazebo looks over the pool and the little rill which feeds it – the perfect place to relax.

agonized over this for a while, ultimately deciding that a straight path would fit best with the straight walls and square plot, but he laid the paving as stepping stones, to allow planting between the slabs, to soften and brighten the line. When the conservatory was finally filled with plants, and with the addition of some handsome cast iron furniture it really was a sanctuary for tired or harassed people who needed to refresh their minds.

THE STREAM AND POND

Geoff called the stream a 'rill'. Well, I told you that he was a romantic. He also called the radio the 'wireless' and the cinema the 'flicks'. But I have to admit that the 'rill' was a lovely feature in the Town Garden. It was fed by a lion head fountain set in the wall, so that the garden was filled with the constant sound of rippling water.

Again it was formed in a straight line, so that it would take the eye of someone sitting in the gazebo directly to the lion's head on the wall opposite. It was constructed in the same way as the stream described on page 164, but in this case, because it was formal and straight, four small, semi-circular bays were built, to take clay pots of irises, which softened the straight lines and added a country touch.

The stream fed a pond, which Geoff designed to surround the gazebo and to give a truly calming effect for the lucky person relaxing inside. Again constructed in the same way as previously described (see page 164), it was graded in depth to accommodate both marginal and deep-water plants and an area of bog garden, as well as providing a small oasis for any wildlife that cared to visit.

THE GAZEBO

This was a feature that Geoff really went to town on, although it did not cost as much as the up-market structures you can find advertised in the glossy magazines. It was made by a fine local craftsman, Peter Wallace of Uppingham in Rutland, who created an elegant masterpiece that fitted its location to perfection. In the corners created by arches below the roof he fitted some delightful wood carvings made by Glynn Mould, a true artist in wood, depicting country symbols – a spider in a web, a few country flowers and a robin. Geoff had strongly held views about most things and one of his passions concerned the need to keep the old country traditions alive by using the skills of people like Peter and Glynn, particularly when they could add such beauty to one's life. Geoff was so taken with the result that he asked Glynn to make him a front door for his house at Barnsdale, which is resplendent with symbols of country life and gardening.

The gazebo was sited on the west side of the plot, facing east, because he

Opposite: The conservatory looked big initially but when the planting was complete it softened into the background.

Acer palmatum.

Anthemis tinctoria.

Dicentra formosa.

wanted it to catch the early morning sun, so that he could sit in it at the best part of the day and listen to the birds entertaining him, see the reflection of the sky in the pond and just enjoy being surrounded by the fresh scents of morning. Of course, if you are unfortunate enough to have to catch the 7.45 a.m. to King's Cross each morning you may feel disinclined to do this, and prefer to sink into your hideaway at the other end of the day with a large Scotch in your hand. In that case you will have to site such a structure in your own garden on the east side, to get the evening sunshine.

THE PATIO
The patio had a curved design, to offset the straight lines of the wall, and it faced south so that it could catch some sunshine for most of the day. For this Geoff used a soft sandstone imitation Yorkstone paving, which blended well with the colour of the walls and provided a hot, reflective surface that would make the very best of any sunshine our mischievous summer threw at us.

In the bed between the curve of the patio and the wall he planted a jumble of cottage garden plants, to spill in cascades of colour over the edge of the patio and give a cheerful, spirit-lifting randomness to the formal lines of the wall. He was careful to choose plants that were heavily scented, to assault the nose and to attract millions of insects.

He set large plant containers around the patio, which looked across the whole garden, so that anybody relaxing there in the sunshine would be surrounded by what Geoff called 'my three-dimensional Arcadia' – drowsy perfumes, trickling water, sensitively blended colours and warm sunshine.

THE PLANTING PLAN
Unlike the cottage gardens' plans, where the planting was largely random, the planting plan for the Town Garden was inspired by the carefully blended and co-ordinated colours originally introduced by Gertrude Jekyll. Next to the pond Geoff used deep purples, reds and blues, with just a splash of orange to brighten their soothing but sombre look. This merged into a square bed on the other side of the path, where the colours were lightened with brighter reds, blues and pinks, carrying the eye round to another square bed which was planted with much brighter yellows, scarlets and greens.

THE PLANTS
As always Geoff began with trees, and here he had a good idea. Many gardens are too small for many trees, especially large species, so Geoff

suggested 'borrowing' them from the neighbours. Often you find that there are already trees or tall plants growing next door, and Geoff felt it was good to plant in a way which complemented what was already there. He had two tall acers growing just outside the walls, so he planted a smaller Japanese maple, *Acer palmatum*, between the two to complete the triangle. He also planted some climbers on the wall behind so that by the time they had grown and hidden the wall the acers would look like a part of his garden. These were *Solanum jasminoides* 'Album', a semi-evergreen climber with small dark green leaves and crisp white flowers from summer right through to November, and *Fremontodendron* 'California Glory', an evergreen wall shrub, which has to be trained, and sports large yellow, saucer-like flowers all summer.

In the sunny, high-walled part of the garden Geoff used plants such as the pineapple broom, *Cytisus battandieri*, which is a tall shrub with silver foliage and large yellow flowers in summer. To attract insects he planted *Euphorbia mellifera*, an evergreen that grows to 90cm–1.25m (3–4ft) and has tiny flowers, heavily scented with a delicious honey smell. He loved *Nepeta* 'Six Hills Giant' because of its lovely spikes of blue flowers, which soldier on all summer, and contrasted it with *Anthemis tinctoria*, a plant with brilliant yellow daisies and scented green foliage, and *Heuchera micrantha* var. *diversifolia* 'Palace Purple', an evergreen gem which flowers all summer, with spires of rich cream flowers.

For the pond and bog garden he planted *Schoenoplectus lacustris* subsp. *tabernaemontani* 'Zebrinus', which is the least invasive of the bulrushes, growing to about 90cm (36in) and having young stems unusually banded in green and white. Geoff could not be without his irises, and used *Iris laevigata*, which has mid-blue flowers in early summer, together with *Lysimachia ciliata*, which has splendid bronze leaves, topped by clear yellow flowers in summer. He also planted *Dicentra formosa*, another of Geoff's firm friends. It has to be protected from frost in spring, but rewards your diligence with delicate, pale green foliage and pale pink flowers early in the year.

Because the garden was small and completely surrounded by a wall it was inevitable that there should be an area of deep shade. Geoff wanted to plant this with ferns, but ferns like not only shade but also damp, and in this area the soil was particularly dry. So, never daunted, he decided to change the nature of the soil. He dug out the space to a depth of about 45cm (18in) and lined the bottom of the hole with old fertilizer bags. These would not retain the water like a butyl liner, but would be enough to keep the soil moist. This particular part of the garden was also close to a water tap, so he determined that he would not change the tap washer often because if it dripped a little his ferns would love it.

Barnsdale, where the Town Garden was built, is naturally quiet, but such a garden could easily be created in a busy town or on a housing estate where, because of its design and the mellow, climber-covered walls, it would be a quiet, private, sweet-smelling sanctuary, filled with colour and light – the perfect place for peace and ease.

The Country Garden

When Geoff conceived the idea for the Country Garden his romantic notions got the better of him again. He had a vision of himself living in a cottage in the woods, where he would make his living coppicing hazel for thatching pegs or burning charcoal. It went back to the days of our youth when we did just that, not actually living in the idyllic cottage that he imagined, but living rough in shelters we had made for ourselves from timbers thatched with bracken. Tracking animals, cooking over open fires and playing small guitars excruciatingly badly, we imagined ourselves variously as the Last of the Mohicans, Canadian backwoodsmen or Australian aborigines. Memories of our early halcyon days never left us and we would bore many a friend with tales of our exploits. I am certain that this is what influenced Geoff, not only in the design of this garden but in the whole paradise garden concept.

Although Geoff imagined the Country Garden as the kind of plot which might be attached to a cottage in a clearing in the woods or some other country place, he wanted to make it reproducible at the back of a council house or on an estate, because that's where most people live and that's where seclusion and peace is most often sought after. To be able to visualize it, he said, it would be necessary to imagine that your house had been transported to the country and you were surrounded by the soft rustle of leaves or by bleating lambs and lowing cattle – not that easy in Barking or Burnley, but a flight of fancy he had already seen manifested in many an amateur garden.

PRIVACY

Privacy was top of Geoff's list of priorities for a garden, not because he believed you should hide your garden from the neighbours but because he believed a garden is a place to hide yourself away when you need those periods of contemplation that restore the spirit.

The Country Garden was bounded by a simple 1.5m (5ft) panel fence, which started life as a hideous orange but was subsequently stained dark green, to blend into the background. This was used partly because the

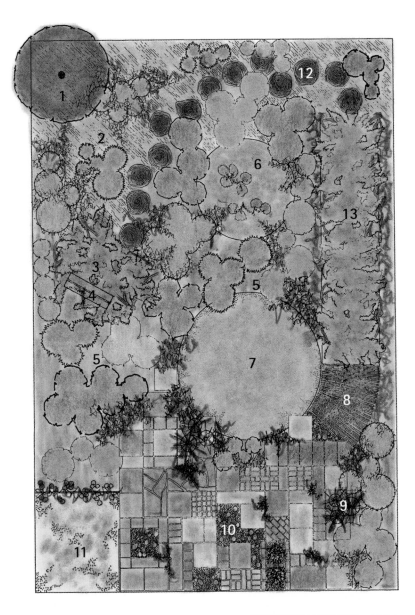

1 *Cercidiphyllum japonicum*

2 Flowery mead

3 Hornbeam arbour (*Carpinus betulus*)

4 Seating

5 Planting

6 Pond

7 Lawn

8 Roofing-tile path

9 Pots

10 Reclaimed paved area

11 Gravel storage area

12 Log stepping stones

13 Nut walk

The little patio in the Country Garden is the perfect place to enjoy its calm and beautiful surroundings.

television programme demanded a 'quick fix' and partly because the garden was so small that a hedge, which Geoff would probably have preferred, would have taken up too much room and robbed the soil of valuable nutrients and moisture.

On one side of the Country Garden he extended the height of the fence, using trellis which he made himself from roofing laths, stained green like the fence and screwed to the existing fence posts. This enabled him to cover it with climbers, which would give him the privacy he sought. He stretched wire along the length of the fence so that the climbers could be tied in, or those that had tendrils could get a hold.

The climbers he chose were *Clematis* 'Etiole Violette', a purple-flowered variety for midsummer, the honeysuckle *Lonicera sempervirens*, which has orange and scarlet flowers, and *Rosa* 'Blush Noisette' which has small flowers and which Geoff grew mainly for its heady scent.

The front fence was a low paling fence that would have sent the important message to the neighbours that he was not trying totally to exclude them. Geoff always felt that if you could not get on with your neighbours you had better move or seek some reliable therapy – or both.

THE PATIO AND THE PAVING

Geoff did not feel it would be in keeping with the Country Garden to lash out mountains of money on materials. Apart from the fact that most of the old countrymen would not have been well off, as always, he was aware of the fact that this must also apply to a lot of young aspiring gardeners today, and these were the majority of his viewers and readers. So he took himself off to the local demolition yard to see what he could find. He came away with a motley assortment of materials that he felt the chap was only too pleased to get rid of – and he paid next to nothing for them. He got some assorted paving stones of different sizes and colours, some engineering bricks, a few cobbles, some roofing tiles and a couple of old clay sewer pipes.

Of course, Geoff had a vision beforehand of what he wanted to do with them, but even if you have no vision, a trip to the demolition yard will often spark off some good ideas – and your garden will become unique, because nobody else will have the same ideas as you. Things you buy there will cost very little and you can always decide what to do with them afterwards, when you have got them home and can cogitate.

The great attraction of the patio in the Country Garden was the random nature of the paving. Geoff interspersed the few paving stones he salvaged with cobbles and bricks, and sunk the clay sewer pipes into the ground to provide planting pockets for attractive plants, like the alpine pratia, *Pratia angulata*, and some thymes, which provided an interesting and

Opposite: The borders in the Country Garden were more informal and rustic than those in the Town Garden, giving a relaxed and tranquil feel to the garden.

aromatic feature. But it was the path that caught my imagination. The inventive old boy set the roofing tiles on edge, so that they made not only a very durable surface, but also a most interesting pattern. He simply set them into a cement base, so that they would stay put and withstand the pressure of the feet of generations of people.

THE NUT WALK

The roofing tile path led into the Nut Walk, which I think was one of the most charming features of the garden. Again Geoff made this in the pursuit of privacy. A tunnel of nut trees growing over arches, it allowed you to walk and talk, or just think, unseen by anybody. I always thought of it as a kind of living cloister and I could imagine Geoff in his monk's habit, pacing back and forth, reading a holy book. On second thoughts, though, Geoff was such a rascal that it is doubtful that he would have passed the monks' entrance exams.

He made the arches using coppiced hazel withies, which are long and supple, and can be easily bent. First he marked out a template for the arch about 2.4m (8ft) tall and he then hammered some pegs into the ground, to follow the shape of the template, with an additional peg at each end to hold the structure in place. He then bent the withies around the pegs and wired the tops together at about 15cm (6in) intervals. He repeated this process until he had enough arches to form his tunnel. He then positioned these at regular intervals along the path, each one next to a short wooden post that he had hammered into the soil earlier. The withies were nailed to the posts to ensure that they were firm and solid. Next he wired horizontal withies to the arches – one just below the arch and one about halfway up the vertical stem. This ensured that the arches were straight, uniform and stable.

The final job was to plant the nut trees. Geoff used hazel (*Corylus*), choosing single-stemmed trees about 1.8m (6ft) tall. When you plant hazelnut trees you must make sure that you buy fruiting varieties and that you have a pollinator, as no hazels are self-fertile. Geoff recommended *C. maxima* 'Gunslebert', which has large cobs of rich flavour. To make the arched tunnel you tie the stems to the withies and in future years cut out the leading shoots of each tree once they have met at the apex of the arch. Side branches can be trained on to the horizontals or, if in the wrong position, cut out. Any suckers should also be pulled out, to retain the shape of the tunnel.

Around its base Geoff planted lady's mantle, *Alchemilla mollis*, a delicate, pale green plant which has the pleasant habit of catching raindrops, so that it glistens after a shower.

MAKING A WITHY ARCH

Geoff made the arches using coppiced hazel withies, which are long and supple, so that they can be easily bent. First he marked out a template for the arch and hammered some pegs into the ground, to the required shape.

The tops were wired together at about 15cm (6in) intervals. Geoff repeated this process until he had enough arches to form his tunnel.

He then positioned these at regular intervals along the path, next to a short wooden post that he had hammered into the soil earlier. The withies were nailed to the posts to ensure that they were firm and solid.

Next the horizontal withies were wired to the arches – one just below the arch and one about halfway up the vertical stem. This ensured that the arches were straight, uniform and stable.

THE ARBOUR

The path through the Nut Walk led inevitably, given Geoff's penchant, to an arbour. Laid in gravel, the path went past the pond, which was made in the way described on page 164. Just past the pond Geoff left behind the formality of the gravel and laid some stepping stones. These he made from sawn rounds of tree trunk, covered with wire netting to prevent people from slipping on them when they were wet. They provided just the right signal that you are approaching an informal, sylvan feature of the garden.

Geoff loved woods and he wanted to make an arbour that reminded him of his idyllic childhood and also surrounded him with the sights and the smells of trees. The arbour was special and rather unusual, in that it is a living arbour, constructed from common hornbeam trees, *Carpinus betulus*.

He started by marking out a circle 2.5m (8ft) in diameter and planted the trees 60cm (24in) apart, with a slightly wider space at the entrance. The trees were tied to a stout stake with a plastic tree tie about 90cm (36in) from the ground. The roof was created simply by pulling the tops of the trees into the centre and tying them together. Once the trees had grown they would be clipped into a perfect dome.

The floor of the arbour was levelled and covered with chipped bark, which makes an ideal base. A small table and a couple of garden chairs completed the furnishings and he had a refuge fit for a king – or a monk.

THE FLOWERY MEAD

Who but Geoff would have called it a flowery mead? I have to admit that I laughed at him when he first described it like that to me, but when it was completed that was just what it was – a flowery mead. I would have called it a wild flower meadow, but it wasn't. In the context of the garden and the ineffable sense of peace it carried with it, it became a flowery mead. No other name would have fitted. Tail between one's legs once more – but I loved him for it.

Wild flower meadows were a delight to Geoff, but he decided that the Country Garden was really too small to do a wildflower meadow justice. It was inevitable that it would be breathtaking for a short time but impossible to keep flowering all through the year. So he decided to plant it with low-growing ornamental grasses in drifts, to provide an attractive background and then to interplant with herbaceous perennials and hardy annuals, which would self-seed. If he chose the right plants this would look like a genuinely ancient flowery mead, but would flower all through the year. I bet those blessed monks wish they'd thought of that!

The grasses he chose were *Acorus gramineus* 'Ogon', which has brilliant yellow leaves, *Milium effusum* 'Aureum', with floppy leaves of soft yellow, turning green with age, *Festuca glauca*, a blue, narrow-leaved grass, all contrasted with *Ophiopogon planiscapus* 'Nigrescens' a grass with black leaves.

Amongst the many plants he chose his favourite were *Papaver nudicaule*, a gloriously prolific and varied poppy that seems to flower endlessly and has single, tissue-paper flowers in pinks, white, cream, yellow and orange; and *Geranium* x *cantabrigiense* 'Biokovo', a long-flowering plant that has pale pink flowers with darker centres. He also used *Trifolium repens* 'Purpurascens', a red clover, which made an ideal foil for the grasses, but must be kept in check as it is a very vigorous grower.

It is perhaps significant that having seen Geoff's Flowery Mead, I swallowed my pride and legged it back home to my garden to make one of my own – and now I have a seat next to it so that I can think about all the things that Geoff taught me and all the good times we had together.

THE WOODLAND WALK

I was once told by one of the Catalyst Television crew, who made *Gardeners' World*, that, as soon as the filming was over and they were disappearing down the drive at Barnsdale, Geoff could be seen hurrying off to his Woodland Walk for a few moments of unwinding after the helter-skelter of

a day's television work. Lynda did not join him for this because she knew that he needed solitude to allow his mind to stop racing and his excitement and enthusiasm to abate. The Woodland Walk was one of the additional *Paradise Gardens* ideas, not incorporated into either of the paradise gardens, simply because it was too big. Geoff loved this place, with its smell of damp leaves, the song of the birds and the dappled light that fell at his feet. He even built a little hut, which he called the Hermitage. It was thatched with bundles of birch twigs and had a small flap in the door, so that he could sit inside and watch the wildlife visiting the pond near by. The insensitive television crew called it 'the Khazi' and were unspeakably rude about its possible uses.

If you have the space for a woodland walk it is a wonderful feature. If you have a little space it is possible to plant a small grove of trees, which will give you almost the same effect. I have done it in my own garden – just

The Hermitage, in which Geoff would sit and quietly watch the wildlife in the woodland and the adjacent pond.

189

Opposite: Part of the
Woodland Walk,
showing one of the
beautiful white-trunked
silver birches, *Betula
utilis*.

with five trees, and, with a seat at one side it makes a very peaceful place to
reflect and ponder.

For the planting of the trees (see pages 16–18), Geoff was very lucky, in
that he already had a magnificent backdrop of mature trees running
alongside his gardens, so he decided to blend the two together, by planting
fairly closely to the established trees, so that they would eventually blend
to form a deep wood and give the feel of a true forest.

There are, of course, a multitude of species that can be used for a
woodland walk, but here are some that Geoff chose at Barnsdale. The
graceful Himalayan birch, *Betula utilis* var. *jacquemontii*, has brilliant white,
peeling bark and long yellow catkins, overflowing with pollen; this is a big
tree, growing to 25m (80ft), but its very open habit means that shade is not
a problem. *Gleditsia triacanthos* 'Sunburst' is a smallish tree that delights the
eye with a splash of dazzling yellow leaves. The elegant *Sorbus* 'Joseph Rock'
has white flowers and a mass of yellow berries which provide a plentiful
supply of food for foraging birds. Stag's horn sumach, *Rhus typhina*, is
another lovely tree, with deeply dissected leaves borne on downy brown
stems, the leaves turning an amazing shade of orange in autumn. But
Geoff's real favourite was the Katsura tree, *Cercidiphyllum japonicum*, which
can grow to about 30 m (100 ft) if not kept in check by pruning, but which
gives a wealth of gifts to the grower – silken bronze leaves in spring,
turning to blue-green in summer and yellow, pink and purple in autumn
as well as a delicious smell of burnt toffee. Geoff always said that when he
died he would like to be buried under such a tree and, sure enough, there
is now one planted next to where he lies in the tiny country churchyard
near Barnsdale.

Underneath the trees he planted shrubs, herbaceous perennials and
bulbs of all kinds. The trees were joined in wedlock with shrubs such as
Hydrangea arborescens 'Annabelle', which luxuriates in a blanket of green-
white flowers in huge rounded heads, and *Deutzia* x *hybrida* 'Mont Rose', a
free-flowering shrub with rose pink flowers in early summer. Two plants
Geoff would not have been without were the comely *Camellia japonica*
'Adolphe Audusson', a compact shrub with large semi-double red flowers
and a real gem, *Sarcococca orientalis*, which brightens up the winter with a
cloud of white, heavily scented flowers, followed by black fruits.

Several varieties of ferns hid quietly in the shadowy, damper parts of the
walk, but where the sun broke through the space was filled with
herbaceous plants such as *Brunnera macrophylla*, which displays small, blue,
forget-me-not-like flowers in May and June; Solomon's seal, *Polygonatum* x
hybridum, with graceful arching branches and white flowers in June; and
Viola odorata, which bears deep purple flowers from February through to

Hydrangea arborescens 'Annabelle', a brilliant white shrub, which brightens the shade of the Woodland Walk.

April. Snowdrops, cyclamen, fritillaria, bluebells, narcissi and aconites carpeted the floor of the walk.

It was small wonder to me that, after the rough and tumble of the demanding work he did, Geoff liked to escape to this special paradise.

THE FINEST AND THE BEST

The *Gardeners' World* television programme *Paradise Gardens* and the associated book of that name were, I believe the most accomplished and imaginative pieces of work that Geoff ever undertook. They were also, sadly, to be his last, but it was typical of Geoff that he quit while he was ahead, and it is perhaps fitting — and oddly but comfortingly prophetic, as is the fact that it should bear that title — that the project encapsulated the essence of his life and his work, expressing all the philosophies that Geoff held most dear.

Both paradise gardens were intensely beautiful and as such a testament to his skill and life's endeavour. Being organic gardens, as was the whole of

Barnsdale, they were in tune with nature and encompassed his belief that life, both animal and plant, is sacred and worthy of respect and reverence. They showed how everybody could create the small sanctuary that he was so keen for them to have – a place to set their minds at rest and to take stock of their world.

The story of the director of the programme is perhaps an interesting reflection of the power of its results. The director was a man called Ray Hough, a lovable, laughing, irreverent cockney with a wicked sense of humour and a complete lack of interest in gardening. He loved the city life, with its pubs and 'caffs', its theatres and cinemas and particularly its football, its odd and eccentric occupants, and its frantic pace. He was completely at home with the bustle and noise, and even rose to the challenge of its hostilities. He did not know one end of a garden fork from another and he had the potential to wreak serious havoc if let loose in anybody's garden. Nevertheless, he was a very fine and creative documentary film maker. He looked upon the job as an interesting one, with lots of artistic possibilities, but just another job; however, he was the kind of person who had an insatiable thirst for knowledge and experience and he soaked up Geoff's skills and wisdom like a sponge. (It is perhaps unkind to mention that that was not all that Ray and Geoff soaked up together.)

The experience of working with Geoff on *Paradise Gardens* changed his life. Ray, the hard-bitten, experienced film maker who had been everywhere and seen everything, gradually realized not only that the message that Geoff was getting across was sincere and valuable, but also that even he could improve the quality of his life by taking some of it on board. Now he has become an avid gardener himself, albeit with a small plot in the centre of London, and he now telephones me, just like I used to ring Geoff, prefacing his conversation with the words, 'Welcome to *Gardeners' Question Time*,' and following with, 'Tone, how do I prune my roses' or 'Is it time to plant my garlic yet?' I love him for it, perhaps because it is one of the nicest compliments I could have about the achievements of my brother.

When Geoff so sadly died all the filming for the programme had been completed, but some of the voice-overs were still to be done, and I was very privileged to be asked to do them on Geoff's behalf. It was an enormous pleasure and release to be able to help finish something that my brilliant brother had so nearly completed – I just hope I did him justice. Both Lynda and I found it hard to watch the programmes when they were screened, but we were both immensely proud to be involved in the final output from such a creative, inventive, witty, generous-hearted and simply good man.

Sorbus 'Joseph Rock'.

The striking bronze *Brunnera macrophylla*.

Camellia japonica.

Barnsdale after Geoff

Barnsdale now is both very different from and much the same as the place it was when Geoff was alive. In some ways it's a little sadder for all of us who knew and loved Geoff, because there is nobody who does not miss his fun and laughter, his incurably silly tricks and his enormous generosity of spirit. In other ways it has become just what Geoff would have wanted: a peaceful and inspiring place for people to come to enjoy the product of his fertile imagination and enterprise, and perhaps to learn some of the old dog's tricks so that they can carry them back to enhance their own gardens.

THE GROWTH OF THE NEW BARNSDALE

When Geoff died, his family decided to open Barnsdale to the public. Not only was it a testament to a man of whom we were all inordinately proud but we wanted in some way to continue the work that Geoff had so successfully begun. We wanted to give the public, who were unable to see Geoff's work at first hand during his life, access to all the ideas and innovations that he had worked so hard to communicate on television.

The idea was never to make Barnsdale into a changeless shrine – the Gracelands of gardening. Geoff would have shrunk in horror at the thought of that. He always said that a garden was an ever-changing thing, evolving as the thoughts and aspirations of the gardener changed. Neither would Geoff have approved of it becoming a theme park. He would have wanted a place where people could come for the gardening, and nothing else. So, whilst there is a muted reminder of Geoff, in the form of a small memorial garden, there are no bouncy castles, no tea towels or mugs and no hot dogs – just a beautiful garden that people can get lost in both physically and mentally.

Nick, Geoff's middle son, now runs the gardens and the nursery at Barnsdale, together with his wife, Sue. Nick is experienced and well qualified to do this. Not only did he work for several years with Geoff, learning his skills, he is also a trained horticulturist, having followed his father to Writtle College to obtain some good qualifications. Sue was Geoff's secretary for many years and, when she was first employed Geoff warned her that she might be asked to do some weeding from time to time – not a thing that a normal businessman would ask of his secretary. But Sue was a country girl, used to farms and horses and gardens, so she didn't bat an eyelid and, sure enough, would spend a good deal of her time on her hands and knees in the garden. In fact she would often boast that she was

195

a better weeder than a secretary. She is also an intelligent, observant person and she watched Geoff as he went about his work, she memorized plant names as she weeded round them, she did bouts of relief work in the greenhouses – and gradually she became a very accomplished gardener in her own right.

When Geoff died, Nick was faced with the task of converting Barnsdale from a television garden to a gardening experience to which he could invite the public. The problems this presented are perhaps not always appreciated by the people who visit, because the vast majority have a smooth, thoroughly enjoyable day and, of course, take all the amenities for granted. Well, why shouldn't they? But Nick, a young man recently deprived of his support and mentor and with little money, had to plan and build car parks, toilets, a coffee shop, tea gardens as well as getting the garden into shape for visitors. A chip off the old block, he stuck to the task, together with Sue and a loyal and industrious staff, and turned the gardens into a matchless experience where visitors can not only spend a day in sublimely beautiful surroundings but also learn from Geoff's timeless skills and imagination.

Nick was very conscious of the need to preserve the atmosphere of peace and serenity that Geoff so loved at Barnsdale, so the number of visitors is carefully restricted to ensure that the gardens do not become overcrowded. In fact they seem to embrace the visitors like old friends, so that they become, like the best old friends, absorbed and unobtrusive. But planning to accommodate 60,000 people a year is a very different kettle of fish to the problems Geoff faced. He reached more people, but they were not all in his back garden.

The first priority was to reorganize the place to receive 120,000 heavy feet, anything up to ten coaches a day and innumerable cars.

So top of the list was the building of car parks and paths round the garden, so that visitors could, as far as possible, enter a mud-free zone. This is not as easy as it sounds because, although some good granite-chip paths were laid in places that had previously been just mud, most of the paths were grass and the replacement of these would have spoiled the gentle, pastoral nature of the gardens. But Nick came up with some green artificial paths, which are laid over the grass and which he has to move laboriously each day so that the grass underneath is not damaged. People still come in pouring rain, girt in wellies and macs, brollies at the ready and stiff upper lips much in evidence, just to see the work of the man they loved to watch – or just loved. On really wet days they may churn up the grass a little, and they are welcome to do so, but each spring, before the gardens are opened again, there is feverish turfing and re-seeding activity to get it back into shape. Geoff would have expected that.

After the paths, the gates, the fences and the signs came all the other accoutrements that go with dealing with large numbers of people – a coffee shop, toilets, stewards to marshal cars, assistants to answer questions and a host of other small but burdensome details.

As well as this Nick had to get the gardens themselves into shape for visitors. Barnsdale is now run differently to the way it was when Geoff ran it – not in terms of the actual gardens or, to any great extent, the layout. The difference is that when Geoff ran it, it was operated exclusively for television and pictorial work so, with a small staff, Geoff tended to concentrate his efforts on the limited areas that were to be used for next week's programme or photograph. Now it *all* has to be kept shipshape, to meet the demands of a discerning and knowledgeable public.

Nick and Sue have worked hard to maintain the spirit of what Geoff stood for and to show visitors the gardens that have become familiar to them through his work on television, but whilst they have kept the gardens much as they were, they have allowed each garden to evolve and change a little.

Lathyrus odoratus
'Geoff Hamilton'.

THE NEW GARDENS

There are also some new gardens. When Geoff was alive visitors were not allowed into Barnsdale. It was Geoff's private garden and his workplace, and it would not have been appropriate. But curious and enthusiastic gardeners were constantly asking to see Geoff's gardens. So he bought another piece of land next to the nursery and on that he, Nick and Adam Frost, Geoff's talented landscape designer, built replicas of the gardens that were, in fact, just over the hedge, for visitors to the nursery to see. Now that Barnsdale is open to the public, Nick is gradually replacing these replicas in the nursery area with new gardens. These are built with a view to designing something that will not only be beautiful but will also be a learning experience for those gardeners who come to Barnsdale in search of ideas and inspiration.

Amongst the new gardens is the Plantsman's Garden, which is filled with a stunning array of unusual plants, to show the alternatives to the normal plants which can be found in every garden. That is not to disparage those normal plants – they are popular because they are good – but it is an attempt to show people the excitement of finding different subjects, which will give them a lot of pleasure to buy and endless joy to live with.

A Knot Garden is being designed, with beds bordered by neatly clipped box, which will live within the gentle sound of rippling water from a brilliant water feature which will provide a soothing background for contemplation.

Viola 'Barnsdale Gem'.

Penstemon 'Geoff Hamilton', bred by Clive and Kathy Gandley.

Rosa 'Geoff Hamilton', bred by David Austin Roses.

Another area has been converted into four small patio gardens, designed to give a range of ideas and inspiration for visitors about to build or refurbish their own patio. With simple but attractive hard landscaping and some exotic plant containers filled with dazzling plants, it is an inspiring experience – but gentlemen be warned: if you let your wife see it she will not let you rest until she has one.

The Penstemon Garden contains an extensive range, propagated from the National Penstemon Collection, and shows visitors the enormous choice of this very fashionable plant that is now available. It has been built on a raised bed, to provide the well-drained conditions these plants prefer. The focal point is a beautiful carmine penstemon, bred by Clive and Kathy Gandley of Cullompton in Devon, who kindly called it *Penstemon* 'Geoff Hamilton' as a tribute to the man and to their happy friendship with him.

Geoff's Mediterranean Garden, which he showed frequently on television, was originally in the courtyard garden close to his house, and this has now been separated from the main garden at Barnsdale. So plans are being laid to build a new one which visitors can see, to give them some ideas about how they can use a hot, dry area that is normally not hospitable for many British plants. It may not follow the exact design of Geoff's original, because of course it will be sited in a different place, but it will embody all Geoff's ideas and principles.

Barnsdale Gardens recently received an award from the Rutland Access Group for providing good facilities for wheelchairs and for people who are not as sprightly as they were, and this sparked the idea of another special garden, designed for people who are less mobile and unable to cope with heavy work. Additionally Sue is currently researching a design for a Japanese Garden, which is expected to be completed early in the new millennium.

In the early days of organic gardening Geoff built an Organic Garden, which saw no chemical sprays or fertilizers. But as for the last years of Geoff's life the whole of Barnsdale was organic, the space devoted to the Organic Garden has now become redundant. So it has been converted into a Wildlife Garden, which demonstrates how to attract birds, butterflies, bees, insects of all kinds and small mammals into the garden, to surround yourself wth the sights, sounds and smells of nature, wherever your garden may be.

Perhaps the most poignant new garden at Barnsdale is Geoff's Memorial Garden, which features Geoff's favourite 'flowery mead' as well as a conventional lawn, in the centre of which is a rose bed filled with the lovely pale pink, cup-shaped rose bred by David Austin Roses and called *Rosa* 'Geoff Hamilton'. The roses can be enjoyed from an unusual bench,

designed and built by Peter Wallace, who built the arbour in the Paradise Garden. Peter gave freely his design and skill, while the small group of staff then working at Barnsdale bought the fine hardwood timber from which it is made.

In the centre of the bed is a unique tribute to Geoff, made by his youngest son Chris. Chris is an artist and a teacher, with a considerable talent in sculpture and ceramics. After Geoff died he determined to use his gifts to make a permanent memorial to his father that would reflect both Geoff's irrepressible spirit and his own love and regard for him. So he set out to do something he'd never attempted before – to make a bust of Geoff from clay, that could eventually be cast in bronze. Like a starving artist in a garret he agonized and slaved at this work, staying awake until the small hours, trying desperately to get it right. Working from photographs this wasn't easy and on one occasion he even asked me to visit him in Hertfordshire – just so that he could look at my face. There was a part he couldn't get right and he needed to see me, Geoff's *doppelgänger*, to give him the inspiration he needed. I sat patiently, the first and last modelling job I have ever done, and eventually with a few skilful touches with his palette knife he achieved the effect he wanted. The finished bust now sitting in Geoff's Memorial Garden is a singular tribute to a singular man.

Part of the Memorial Garden built by the HDRA in 1998 in memory of Geoff and his work to promote organic gardening.

Seaton Meadows in Rutland, bought by Plantlife partly with donations from people who wished to pay tribute to Geoff's work.

NEW PLANTS

Barnsdale today is home to a number of plants named after Geoff. In addition to *Penstemon* 'Geoff Hamilton' in the Penstemon Bed and *Rosa* 'Geoff Hamilton' in Geoff's Memorial Garden, there is a superb blue and white lupin called *Lupinus* 'Barnsdale' dedicated to him by Woodfield Brothers of Stratford; an elegant magenta sweet pea named after him by Diane Sewell; and a viola called *Viola* 'Barnsdale Gem', which was a sport that Geoff found in the garden and propagated from a single plant and is now stocked by the nursery. All the plants dedicated to Geoff have been portrayed as botanical paintings (such as those on pages 197–8) by my wife, Carol, a trained horticulturist, who worked for Geoff for seventeen years. Carol had no apparent talent before Geoff's death, but afterwards, almost as if he was guiding her hand, she developed a significant skill, and her paintings, many of which hang at Barnsdale, are now much in demand.

GEOFF'S WORK LIVES ON

Barnsdale is of course not just the place where Geoff created his garden: it is also the place where he conceived and ran his campaigns, the base from which he fought for the causes he cared about. Thanks to Geoff's wife Lynda, and others, much of this work lives on after him.

A resourceful and courageous lady, Lynda is committed to continuing the work that Geoff began, which she does with a tenacity and determination not quite so necessary when Geoff was alive. For example, she is now a vice-president of Plantlife, the charity dedicated to the preservation of wild flowers and their habitats. Plantlife was one of the causes that Geoff felt most passionately about, and he campaigned shoulder to shoulder with them, first to try to persuade gardeners not to use peat and then to try to stop the depredations of big business, who were demolishing beautiful limestone pavements, full of unique wildlife, in the pursuit of profit (see page 160). As a result of Geoff's campaigning work to publicize the cause, and with money that was contributed by generous viewers and readers after his death, Plantlife was able to buy Winskill Stones in North Yorkshire, and it is now a protected reserve, dedicated to Geoff's memory.

Geoff was also unflagging in the promotion of the work done by Sustrans, an organization devoted to the installation of cycle tracks through the length and breadth of Britain. In recognition of this Sustrans has installed a seat on the Taff Trail, in the Brecon Beacons, close to where he died on the cycle ride that was to have taken him to open the trail, so that people can contemplate his memory.

Lynda supports and promotes all this work tirelessly, spending many hours lobbying, cajoling and persuading people to continue to support the work that Geoff was so passionate to pursue.

She also occasionally visits Seaton Meadows in Rutland, one of the last flood meadows left in England, which was also bought by Plantlife after receiving further generous donations from Geoff's followers. It's a lovely meadow, rich with the kind of wild flowers that are no longer seen in most meadows, because it has never been intensively farmed and, whilst it has not been removed from agricultural use, it is managed in a way that will ensure that the plants survive as long as Plantlife, or Lynda, are alive.

Lynda also administers the work of Geoff Hamilton's New Gardeners Foundation. This is a charity which was set up at the instigation of Tony Laryea, the head of Catalyst Television who made *Gardeners' World* and all Geoff's series for the BBC in the later years of his career. Not only did he devote many hours of tedious administration to the setting up of the charity, but he also put together a compilation video of Geoff's work and very generously donated it to the Foundation, as a means of raising income. Tony Laryea is a perceptive and sensitive man who knew of Geoff's desire to help talented young people wishing to follow a similar career path to his own, so he suggested that the money should be used to finance needy students through horticultural courses at Writtle, Geoff's old college. Lynda beavers away at selling hundreds of copies of the video to garden centres, the RHS and many other places. It is also on sale at Barnsdale directly or by mail order. Incidentally, Writtle College has

This captivating bust of Geoff, executed by his youngest son Chris, now stands in the Memorial Garden at Barnsdale.

named a hall of residence after Geoff and Cor van Hage, his first boss, has named one of the rooms in his giant garden centre at Great Amwell in Hertfordshire 'The Geoff Hamilton Room'.

Additionally Lynda has appeared on television and in the press, promoting the principles that Geoff believed in so passionately. Also, much to her joy, she is visited, written to, telephoned constantly by Geoff's old colleagues, from the BBC, from Catalyst and from his publishers and frequently by the people he worked with or interviewed – all wanting to maintain contact with one half of a quite unique couple.

Geoff's commitment to the organic cause is immortalized in a most impressive and moving tribute to Geoff organized and built by HDRA. Alan and Jackie Gear, directors of HDRA, together with Bob Foreman, their curator – and the fount of all knowledge about all things organic – built a magnificent Paradise Garden in memory of Geoff and the work that he had done to promote organic gardening. It was opened formally in June 1999, by Lynda, and the opening was attended by a glittering, though somewhat damp array of celebrities, because it rained cats and dogs all day. I think Geoff had judged that the plants were under-watered, so he decided to put things right. It would be typical of him to put the well-being of the plants before the importance of the occasion. This sensational garden, designed by Isabelle van Groeningen and Gabriella Pape of Land Art, is now a permanent memorial to Geoff's work, and it could hardly be in a more fitting place or cared for by a more fitting group of people.

GEOFF'S LEGACY

It is not given to many to leave behind the kind of legacy that Geoff left. He had so much impact on the world of gardening, persuading millions with his gentle wit and easy-going, practical style that a world of wonderment and the deepest satisfaction awaited them just outside the back door. That he did so is manifested by the visitors to Barnsdale, who are a constant delight and joy, coming as they do with affectionate memories of Geoff's many triumphs – and his few gaffes – and just revelling in their association with his work.

And they come in their thousands. From March to November the gardens are full of people with notebooks, people with magnifying glasses, people with cameras – and no small number of people with a tear on their cheek. For Geoff's spirit can still be felt in his beloved garden, walking in the woodland glades and indulging in his 'admiring time' in his arbours. Perhaps it is in the nature of a garden that, just as one can rely on the perpetual re-emergence of its plants and animals, it embraces the soul of the person who created and tended it and some part of them remains to continue its stewardship. I should like to think so – but then I have inherited the romantic gene just like Geoff.

And what of Geoff's legacy to me? Well, as you would expect, I miss my brother like crazy, as any person robbed of a lifelong friend would and, as I have said many times before, I just long for him to walk through my front door (he never knocked), plonk himself in my chair and say, 'Glass of red wine, please', as was his habit. But I know he won't and I content myself with my lifelong memories and with the company of my wife Carol who worked for Geoff from the beginning of Barnsdale, and Lynda, both of whom share my feelings about Geoff and both of whom can still laugh at his japes and his very silly jokes.

What he left me was not only some wonderful memories but also a greater intimacy with my garden and knowledge of how to nurture it, which I would never have had without him. If ever I had occasion to ask for his help he would begin by moaning and groaning, protesting and posturing, as though I had asked him to sacrifice his all. But I knew that he was just squeezing the last bit of fun he could get out of the situation and eventually he would say, 'OK, I'll come and help, but remember I work only in a strictly supervisory capacity. You have to do the labouring.' So it was Geoff who showed me how to lay paving and build walls and construct steps. It was Geoff who showed me how to prune roses and fruit trees and how to lay turf. It was Geoff who led me away from humdrum vegetables and introduced me to celeriac and fennel and globe artichokes. In fact it was Geoff who made me into the gardener I am today – still humble by his standards, but sometimes congratulated and always deeply, deeply satisfied.

And of course, it was Geoff who gave me the inspiration to write this book. I hope and trust that if you have enjoyed it you will go out and try some of the ideas and plants that inspired him. If as a result you get from your garden just an atom of the joy that he got from his, not only will you have an enriching and uplifting experience but you will have fulfilled Geoff's dearest wish – to share his knowledge so that others could find happiness in helping nature on its way.

The author taking a break to enjoy his own garden.

Index

Acknowledgements

My thanks must go to the following people, without whose care and professionalism this book would never have seen the light of day:

Lynda, Geoff's wife, whose painstaking research work and tireless delving through Geoff's past work went far beyond the call of duty.

Anne Askwith, my brilliant editor, who completed a tiresome job without recourse to alcohol or psychiatric therapy. Without her attention to detail, which enabled her to pounce on all my stupid mistakes, and her seemingly boundless literary and gardening knowledge I would have produced this book several years later. Prue Bucknall, the designer, and Mel Watson, the picture editor, who worked together to produce a design that went far beyond my expectation and did more than justice to my own humble literary skills.

Steve Hamilton, Geoff's eldest son and my errant nephew, who is responsible for most of the pictures. It took only mild applications of the heavy Victorian father approach to get them and it was more fun working with Steve, a man of gigantic creative ability, than I can really describe. I am very proud to have his pictures associated with my text. Nick and Sue Hamilton, who run Barnsdale Gardens and who have given me invaluable advice and support, as well as the run of the gardens for research purposes.

Celia Kent, Headline's Managing Editor, and Louise Rothwell, Production Controller, were the power-house behind the production of the book and I owe a lot not only to their professional skills but also to their amazingly uplifting enthusiasm and good humour.

My great gratitude goes to Heather Holden-Brown, Headline's Non-fiction Director and big cheese, who originally kicked off the idea for the book. She was also an enormous source of encouragement during the production of the book and has a remarkable knack of leaving you with a feeling that it's all going well.

Finally I must thank my wife Carol, who fed me cups of coffee and sandwiches in a seemingly endless stream, but who also listened patiently to every page as I wrote it, made the wisest of suggestions where they were needed and helped me enormously with her considerable horticultural knowledge.